The Univ

- Hidden Knowledge

By

Cheyenne Angel

ISBN: 9781916696433

Table Of Contents

INTRODUCTION

Connecting with a Conscious Universe

"If you want to find the secrets of the universe, think in terms of energy, frequency, and vibration." – Nikola Tesla

At the beginning of the modern age, it was believed that what we now know as the solar system was the entire universe. This was a widely held belief, with many scientists and astronomers of the time believing that the Earth was the center of the universe and that the sun, stars, and other planets revolved around it. This view of the universe was turned on its head by Nicolaus Copernicus, who proposed a heliocentric model of the solar system in which the Sun was the center. This allowed for a much more accurate view of the solar system and universe, and it was soon accepted by most of the scientific community. Over the centuries, the solar system has come to be seen as part of a much larger universe, with a vast array of galaxies and stars. It has become increasingly clear that our solar system is just one part of a much larger and more complex universe, and that there are many more galaxies, stars, and planets out there waiting to be discovered

By the end of the 19th century, it was clear that the solar system was a part of the larger galaxy. And this was a huge milestone, as it meant that if we come from anywhere, we come from the galaxy. This was even more significant when we realized that the galaxy is all there is. That is the whole universe. Therefore, if we come from the universe, we come from the galaxy. Our origins in this vast universe become even more meaningful when we consider that the galaxy is all that is.

It was only recently that we discovered that our Milky Way galaxy is just one of millions of billions of galaxies in the universe. This realization has changed our perception of our place in the universe, allowing us to see that we are part of something much bigger and more complex than we ever imagined. Our knowledge of the universe is constantly expanding and changing as we discover more and more of its secrets. As we continue to explore, our vision of the universe grows ever larger, and we come to understand our place in it more deeply.

Where do the stars come from if we come from the stars? We, humans, come from this universe, but where did this universe come from? This is a question that has been asked for centuries and is now being discussed more and more. While this universe has always been here in some form or another, it has not always been in its current state. It has evolved over time, continuing to change and grow. Scientists have studied its origin and are still searching for answers to this question. It is clear, however, that this universe is a complex and ever-changing entity, and its origin remains one of the greatest mysteries of the cosmos.

The Big Bang is the most widely accepted theory for the origin of the universe, and it is estimated that this enormous event happened around 80.3 billion years ago. This monumental cosmic event is the source of all that we can observe in the universe today. It is thought to have created the galaxies, stars, and planets that make up the cosmos, and even the atoms, molecules, and other particles that make up the matter that we are familiar with. The Big Bang is also thought to have created the laws of physics that govern our universe, allowing it to evolve and change. All in all, it is

is a concept that has long been studied and discussed by many scientists, including the renowned Albert Einstein. He believed that when we truly understand and take these laws seriously, we come to the realization that there must be a great mind or spirit behind them. This is because these laws are coherent and consistent with one another. They are not random or arbitrary, but rather they are based on some fundamental principles that guide our understanding of the universe. It is this great mind, or spirit, that is responsible for the existence of these laws and the coherent order that they bring to our lives. The spirit behind the laws of nature is something to be admired and respected, as it is this great spirit that allows us to understand and explore the world around us.

They create an observable, intelligible universe. We are part of that intelligible universe, and we have co-created that universe with the laws that were born at the same time that we were born. When was this?

Now we enter the deepest mysteries.

The Big Bang is thought to be the origin of the observable, intelligible universe that we are a part of. This is a moment that is shrouded in mystery, as we cannot know what existed before this critical moment.

We may never know what existed before an incredible event that has shaped the universe as we know it today.

The Tao, the quantum vacuum, the unified field, the source, and the Absolute. In the deepest dimension of reality, there is a unified field that holds all the potential for creation. This field is the source of all life, and it is where we come from. It is the place where all the physical laws of the universe are encoded, and where all the possibilities of future creation are stored. This source is the origin of life, and it is from this source that all of us have sprung. It is from this source that we have all come and to this source that we will all return. This is the ultimate source of our being, and this is where we must look if we want to understand the true nature of our existence. We encompass the cosmos. We are children of the cosmos.

We are part of a grander journey, a quest for knowledge and understanding of our place in the universe. We are alive with possibility, with the power to create and shape our own destinies. We are part of a greater mystery, a mystery that may never be fully understood, but one that can be explored and embraced.

We have evolved over time, from a single-cell organism to a species that has the capacity for consciousness, and the ability to contemplate our place in the universe. Our consciousness reflects the deeper dimension from which all things have come. It is from this place that the laws of nature that govern the universe are derived. What we have become reflects this deeper dimension, our consciousness being the embodiment of it. This is who we are, and this is what we will become. We will form a greater understanding of ourselves and the universe and use our newfound knowledge to benefit humanity.

The law of nature the Big Bang, but speculation suggests that it may have been a field of possibility, a place where anything that could possibly come to pass was able to exist. It is also possible that before the Big Bang, there was an intelligence, some sort of cosmic mind, that held all of the potential of the universe within it. Whatever existed before the Big Bang, we can only guess at its nature and its purpose. The Big Bang was an event like no other, and its impact on the universe cannot be understated.

In Christianity, the concept of the "Word" is central to the faith. According to the Bible, "In the beginning was the Word, and the Word was with God, and the Word was God" (John 1:1). This concept of the Word has been interpreted in various ways, but the idea is that the Word was a creative force in the universe. It is often seen as a representation of the creative power of God.

In Eastern religions, this concept of a powerful creative force is also present. Buddhism, for example, speaks of the "Dharma," which is an eternal truth that exists beyond the material world. In Hinduism, the concept of "Brahman" is used to refer to a formless, supreme being that is the source of all creation. In Taoism, the Tao is the ultimate principle of the universe, from which all things arise.

These concepts of the Word, Dharma, Brahman, and Tao all point to a single, underlying truth: that the universe is composed of a single, all-encompassing energy or power. This power is the source of all creation and is the ultimate reality. It is this power that lies at the heart of these Eastern and Christian religions and serves as a reminder of our interconnectedness with the universe.

The universe is a mysterious and wondrous place, and it can be a source of great joy and inspiration. Through science, we can better understand the physical laws that govern our universe, while mysticism can give us insight into the spiritual forces that shape it. Together, science and mysticism can help us to gain a better understanding of the universe and ultimately a better understanding of ourselves.

Vibrations of a certain frequency, phase, and magnitude create structures that seemingly have a material presence. When these vibrations come into phase, they form a harmonious connection that is responsible for these structures. The same vibrations are also responsible for the stability of these structures, as they help them to remain in place. Furthermore, these vibrations can cause the structures to move in unison, forming a cohesive unit. This phenomenon can be found in the natural world, from the movement of electrons to the motion of galaxies. Thus, it is no surprise that the same concept can be seen in the structures created by vibrations.

Over a century ago, renowned astronomer James Jeans made the bold statement that the universe was more akin to a great thought than a great machine. As we have continued to explore the universe, delving into its most minute details, it is becoming increasingly apparent that Jeans' words were prophetic. Our investigations have revealed that the universe is not a mechanical structure but instead appears to be comprised of information that can be understood. This universe is, in effect, a manifestation of a great thought, deeply embedded in its fabric.

50 years ago, the concept of mainstream science was much different than it is today. We see the same

concepts and theories being taught in universities today, but if we really contemplate questions such as "Who are we" and "Where do we come from," we must go beyond what is taught in mainstream science. This is where quantum science comes in. Quantum science recognizes that the world is a quantum system, and that is a very different concept from what was taught in times past. This new, quantum science is necessary to truly understand the questions of our origin and existence.

Max Planck's statement that "there is no such thing as matter in the universe" is a bold one. It suggests that the very foundation of physical reality is not solid, but rather a set of vibrations held together by a force. This force is what creates the atom and the molecules, and the super-molecular objects that make up the universe. This is a fascinating concept, and it is one that has been explored for centuries by great thinkers. In recent years, this idea has been explored in even more detail, as scientists have gained a greater understanding of the structure of the universe.

The many things that we can observe and touch in the physical world are all forms of vibration acting together. As Max Planck famously said, these vibrations are held together by a force, a cosmic intelligence that binds the protons, neutrons, and electrons together. This intelligence is what allows us to create and observe the complexity of the physical world. It is this cosmic intelligence that gives us the ability to understand and appreciate the beauty of the universe. We must never take for granted the wonders of this cosmic intelligence that holds us all together.

What we find instead is energy in the form of vibration, and this energy is the basis of all life, the source of all existence. This vibration is the origin, the source, of all things. It is the foundation of the physical world and the spiritual one, the source of both energy and matter.

We are not merely solid material bodies but are instead a collection of vibrations that interact with each other in a complex system. This system is known as an attractor, which is the term used by science to describe the behaviour of a system. This means that the universe is not random, but is instead shaped and formed by the interactions between its components. As a result, we are more than just solid material bodies; we are part of a larger system that affects how we behave and how the universe behaves as a whole.

We are slowly beginning to unravel the mysteries of the remarkable universe we inhabit, and what is becoming increasingly apparent is the fact that all things are connected and act in unison. Every atom, every star, every organism, and every force are connected, each influencing and being influenced by the others in a vast web of interconnectedness.

How we come in - to think that we come from beyond is an intriguing concept. It can be easily illustrated by considering a game like poker, chess, or any other. The laws of the game are already set and you don't play with the laws. Instead, you play within the framework that the laws provide and their purpose is to guide the game. The laws act as a set of instructions, dictating the rules and the way that the game can be played. In the same way, the laws of nature may act as a set of instructions that dictate the way the universe works and how we can interact with it. It is an intriguing concept to think that from beyond, the laws of nature have been set in place and we are merely playing the game.

The laws of nature are the same for both the novice and the grand master in chess. They are fundamental to the universe and are not part of the game itself. Instead, they are what governs the game. They are eternal and unchanging, having been present since the birth of the universe and likely to remain in place until the end of time. As such, they are the backbone of the chess game and all others, providing the structure and rules that all must abide by.

It is becoming increasingly clear that this universe is not permanent, and that it is subject to a higher will and intelligence that directs its evolution. This is an idea that has been present in religion and spirituality for some time, but it is only relatively recently that it has been recognized by science. This recognition is leading to a deeper understanding of the workings of the universe, and the ways in which it is constantly changing and evolving. As we come to terms with this, it brings with it a newfound appreciation of the beauty and complexity of the universe, and the fact that it is ever-changing.

It all hangs together; this evolution is not random, not just one darned thing after another. As philosophers used to say not so long ago, the universe is not just a sequence of unrelated events, but instead is an ordered progression from chaos to order. We as humans are also part of this progression. Our consciousness and our bodies are both expressions of this evolution. Through our actions and our thoughts, we are part of the grand journey of the universe as it goes from chaos to order. We contribute to the progress and development of this journey, and with each step, we help create the ordered universe we live in today.

Tropism is a fascinating phenomenon that exists in the animal and plant kingdoms, as well as in the universe as a whole. It is the tendency for something to move or grow in response to an external stimulus, such as the sun or a particular scent. This same tropism applies to us as humans, and even to the most basic forms of life, such as bacteria.

Our instincts and our very being are also characterized by tropism. We are always being pulled in a particular direction, be it towards a goal or away from danger. In fact, the same is true of all of evolution. Every element of life, from plants to animals, works together to create a holistic and unified system. This is why tropism is so important, and why it is so crucial that all elements of the universe move in harmony with each other. With each organism moving in the right direction, the world is able to thrive and evolve.

In human life, and in the life of any living system, it is essential to work together in order to maintain existence. We can think of it as a quantum coherent system, in which every part is vital to the functioning of the whole. Without cooperation between the elements of this system, life would cease to exist. This same principle applies to us, as if we are healthy and normal, we are part of a collective drive that works to sustain life. Every individual has the responsibility to do their part in order to ensure the longevity of the system.

We obey it, we live it, and we express it. Intuitive people and indigenous cultures have long known and understood this drive, even if they can't verbalize or conceptualize it. With our ability to conceptualize, put together and interpret things, we are interpreting this drive as a drive for power. However, this interpretation is often misguided, misrepresenting the true nature of this drive. We must take care to understand the true meaning of this drive and not succumb to the temptation of power.

However, this does not mean that competition is the only way to go about life. We are more than capable of recognizing and respecting the inherent oneness of all life in the universe. We must understand that this oneness does not mean that we are all the same, but rather that we are all connected and should treat each other with respect. Instead of viewing other people, creatures, and life forms as competition, we should strive to recognize and honor the interconnectivity between us all. We should not be so quick to perceive competition and violence as the only way to go, but instead, take the time to understand the importance of interconnectedness and oneness. This is the only way to truly progress as a species and move forward in harmony.

We are a part of an ever-evolving universe, both in terms of life and consciousness. To truly recognize this vast cosmic journey is a great challenge for us. To re-cognize this truth requires us to look beyond the knowledge of classical and traditional cultures and to seek out the hidden wisdom of the Mystery Schools. Through this, we can come to a greater understanding of our place in the universe and our connection to all that is.

The challenge of understanding the world around us is a difficult one. We are often influenced by our own beliefs and experiences, and it can be difficult to interpret things in an unbiased way. This means that what we believe can often shape the way we perceive certain things. This is an interesting phenomenon and it can lead to misinterpretations and invalid ideas. We are free to interpret things however we choose, but it is important to remember that our own beliefs can sometimes get in the way of understanding reality. It is up to us to challenge our own preconceptions and strive to have an unbiased view of the world.

We stand at the edge of an evolutionary process, one we have helped to build and shape, but now it is in question whether it can stay on that path. The instability that has come with it is not a bad thing, however, because, without instability, there can be no progress or chance for change. It is through this period of instability that we can push forward and create a new world. We can create new opportunities and possibilities that were not there before. We can make a difference and create a better future for ourselves and for generations to come. So, let us embrace the instability and use it to our advantage. Let us create a new future, one that is better than the one we have now.

Progress is inevitable. When the current situation becomes unsustainable, we are forced to find a new way forward or risk facing extinction. This is the situation we are in today - a moment where we must choose to either adapt and evolve or face the consequences of our inaction. The choices we make today will determine the future of our world. We must ensure that we make the right ones, or risk becoming part of the ever-growing list of species that have gone extinct due to human interference. We must seize this opportunity to move forward and make meaningful change, or risk facing an uncertain future. The stakes are high, but the potential rewards are even higher. Let us move forward with courage and conviction and make the best of this unique moment in history.

The great overwhelming majority of species on this planet have become extinct. This is a sobering realization that highlights the fragility of life on Earth. The human species is not so old in the grand scheme of things- as a conscious species, we have been around for around 50,000 years, and as a biological species, perhaps 3 million to 3.5 million years. However, the power that we now have through technology, the ability to reason, interpret, and make choices, is recent and brings with it great responsibility. We have the potential to cause great destruction to the planet and its species, but we also have the potential to reverse the damage and make the world a better place. The power is in our hands.

We have the ability to act on our interpretations, however misguided they may be. This presents great danger, as freedom is a double-edged sword. On one hand, it allows us to pursue our greatest values and ideals, but it also allows us to pursue our worst. If we are not careful and do not take the time to consider the implications of our actions, the results can be disastrous. We must strive to use our freedom responsibly and judiciously, so that it can be a force for good, rather than a source of destruction.

Ultimately, there is one consciousness; a single, unified source of all that exists in the universe. This is an optical illusion to think of consciousness as residing separately in each of us. We are one mind; one unified consciousness, each of us connected to the same source. This same source, this same mind, is responsible for creating the atoms and molecules, the amoeba and the plants, the algae and the complex organisms, and societies of intelligent life. It is this same source that binds us all together, that is the foundation of the universe, and that can be accessed by each of us to understand our place within it. We are all connected, and we are all part of the same consciousness.

It is the drive towards oneness and the drive towards wholeness that is the source of all things. This drive is not only physical but also mental. As Alfred North Whitehead puts it, all actual entities are subject to both a physical and a mental pull. This drive towards oneness and wholeness is what drives the universe, and it is this energy that creates the systems we see in existence, from the simplest to the most complex. This drive is what creates the beauty and harmony of the world, and it is this drive that binds us all together. It is this drive that pushes us towards our highest potential, and it is this drive that unites us in our shared journey towards oneness and wholeness.

Mysticism is the best guess that we have in science as to how our mind operates, even when the brain is turned off. This is supported by evidence from near-death experiences, where people often report having vivid, conscious experiences while their bodies were clinically dead. For example, some report seeing a bright light or having a sensation of floating outside of their body. Other evidence for the existence of a mental pull beyond the physical comes from the study of Quantum Mechanics. According to this field, all things are actual entities, and they all have a mental pull, as well. This suggests that our minds exist beyond the boundaries of the physical world, and can interact with it even when the physical body is no longer functioning.

The evidence for this is manifold today, from near-death experiences to Quantum Mechanics.

This suggests that our minds are much more powerful and complex than previously thought, and are capable of much more than just the physical body. This is why mysticism remains an important and valid field of study, as it helps us to understand how our minds operate in ways that science has yet to understand.

In the same way, modern concepts can be explained fairly well now because of the concept of cosmic consciousness, which is similar to a hologram. A hologram is a system of information in which every part is contained within each other part. For instance, the totality of information contained within the hologram creates the image. This is a scientific fact that can be demonstrated; every small part of the hologram contains the entirety of the information. This is similar to cosmic consciousness, which is the idea that all of the information contained within something is contained within each individual part of that same thing.

This cosmic consciousness is present in all of us, and it is distributed information. It is something that we receive and can decode, and the brain is the tool that helps to make it perceivable. But it is important to note that this consciousness is not something that we create, it is something that is already there. It is ever-present and all-encompassing, and it is through our brains that we are able to access and understand it. This cosmic consciousness is something that is unique to each individual and an understanding of it can help us to better understand ourselves and the universe around us.

Modern times have made a big mistake in assuming that all of our experiences are solely derived from our five senses. In reality, there is much more to our experiences than what our senses can provide us with. We have experiences known as transcendental experiences, which refer to experiences that go beyond the senses. To gain a deeper understanding of these experiences, there is a growing field of research known as transcendental, transpersonal psychology, and psychiatry. This field of study has been devoted to exploring the elements of consciousness that cannot be derived from sensory information. Through this research, we can gain a better understanding of the transcendental experiences that we have and the true potential of our consciousness.

Near-death experiences, out-of-body experiences, and spontaneous intuitions are phenomena that cannot be explained by rational or sensory-produced ideas. These experiences often arise in the hypnogogic state, a period of consciousness that lies between sleep and wakefulness. Such states can be induced by meditation, hypnosis, and lucid dreaming.

Meditation is a powerful practice that allows us to tap into the collective consciousness and connect with the holographic nature of reality. When we come to meditation, we are not only connecting to ourselves but to all other beings and forms of life.

We are accessing a deeper understanding of our interconnectivity and the powerful energy that surrounds us. This energy is not only within us and between us, but throughout the entire universe. By coming to meditation, we are allowing ourselves to open up to the power of this collective consciousness and the expansiveness of our being. As we explore the depths of this connection, we are reminded of our place in the world and how we are all part of a larger whole.

We are part of the consciousness of our predecessors, and it is unclear whether we are part of the experience of those who have gone before us, or part of the experience of those who will come after us. But one thing is certain, the past is part of the present. Everything that happens to us is informed by the past, and all of us are part of a larger hologram. The future is a probability, but the past is a certainty. We are all part of the same narrative, and the knowledge and wisdom of our predecessors live on in us, no matter what the future may hold.

Our Earth system cannot operate as a plurality of conflicting elements. We are seeing this now, with so many people and nations fighting each other in an effort to protect their own interests. But this is not the way forward. We cannot hope that something positive will come out of all this conflict, something that will maintain the system.

When we talk about 'system', it goes beyond energy and matter. It encompasses the web of life, its various interconnections, and the global quantum system that makes this planet the unique and beautiful place it is. Everyone has a part to play in this system, and when we work together, we can ensure that the Earth's system remains healthy and functioning. We must strive to move away from conflict and towards collaboration so that we can ensure a better future for all.

We have an innate understanding of the need to unify and work together, and this is something that can be seen in our species across the board. We can look to the teachings of Carl Jung for further evidence of this idea, as he believed in the concept of the Unus Mundus, or one world, one consciousness. We can use this as our guide, as it is something we all have inside of us, something that has been passed down through the generations and is essential to our survival. Every child, every animal, and every human being has this same inner wisdom, and this can be a source of strength, unity, and understanding.

The power of the quantum is vast, and it is time to take it seriously and use it to our advantage. What we do now can have a profound effect on our future, and understanding the quantum is the key to unlocking our potential.

The implications of this knowledge are far-reaching, as it helps us to understand the underlying mechanisms of the universe and our place in it. By recognizing the power of holotropic consciousness, we can begin to unlock the secrets of reality and find ways to live in harmony with our surroundings. It is only by understanding the power of holotropic consciousness that we can truly begin to comprehend the role of the universe in our lives.

One could say that this is not a religion in the classical sense. It is more of a spiritual path, a way of life, and a set of beliefs and practices that are shared by a group of people. It is close to some Eastern religions, such as Buddhism and Taoism, but it also has similarities to the Old Testament and the teachings of Jesus. Jesus taught love, oneness, and the pursuit of spiritual enlightenment as the primary goals of life. This spiritual path is not focused on the worship of a single deity, but rather on the pursuit of personal growth and inner peace. The goal is to become more aware of the connection between all things and to live a life of peace, understanding, and love.

We have the power to create a stronger, more unified community right here on Earth. We are all connected, part of the same living, breathing organism, and together, we can bring about meaningful change. We need to strive to create a community that is less vulnerable to conflict, one that is more inclusive and empowering of all. We need a community that is sustainable and that works in harmony with nature.

We can make this happen with our collective efforts. We can become more aware of our interconnectedness, and our responsibility to the planet and its inhabitants. We can learn to communicate and cooperate better so that we can better understand each other and create a shared vision for our future. We can come together to create a society that is more just and equitable, and one that respects the natural environment.

Together, we can create a community that is stronger and more unified, one that is capable of transforming into something better, something more beautiful. This is our opportunity to create a new kind of community, one that is truly built on love, understanding, and respect. This is our chance to make a real, lasting difference in the world.

1

Chapter One

The Powerful ENERGY in The Universe

"For what lies inside the human being is the whole spiritual cosmos in condensed form. In our inner organism, we have an image of the entire cosmos."
— Rudolf Steiner

The study of the magnetic powers of the Sun is an important endeavour that can help us better understand the seasons and the forces that affect our environment. The four seasons of winter, summer, spring, and fall are deeply intertwined with the magnetic factor in the air. We can use astronomy to explain the physical phenomenon of these seasons as it relates to the rotation and revolution of the Sun and planets. Through this study, we can gain insight into the magnetism of the Sun and how it influences our lives and the world around us. This should lead to a better understanding of the power of the Sun and its effects on our environment.

Our universe is made up of planets, stars, and galaxies that are constantly in motion. But each of these planets is much more than just a rocky sphere orbiting around a star. Each one is a field of magnetic energy, and this energy is what we call air. It is this air that flows through our atmosphere and provides us with breathable air. This air is also responsible for the protection of our planet, as it helps to reduce radiation levels and keep the planet cool. The air is also responsible for the weather, as it carries moisture and heat from one place to another. Without this air, life on Earth would be impossible. We owe a great debt of gratitude to the air that surrounds us, as it is essential for our very existence.

Air is so much more than just a scientific definition. It is a substance, an integral part of our environment and existence. We know that air transmits signals, allowing us to watch all kinds of programs on television. But air is more than just a signal, it is an essential factor in our lives, playing a major role in the climate and conditions that we live in. We are incredibly lucky to have air in our lives, and it is important to recognize the importance it has in sustaining us.

We have learned from television that the air transmits various kinds of programs at the same time. Each program remains distinct and separate, as though it is running in its own channel or circuit. This means that they can overlap and inter-lap, and even a dozen programs can be broadcast at the same time. This is a remarkable testament to the power of technology and the potential of broadcasting.

We may turn on and off television programs, but what is actually being broadcast through the air is not what we see on our screens. The murder we observe on television is not the same as what is transmitted through the air, as it is not visible in this form. Instead, what is sent through the air is a vibration, which when received at a theatre, home, or other location, is then turned into what we observe on the screen. Therefore, while we may be able to turn on and off television programs, the actual transmission through the air is not what we see on the television screen.

The concept of murder on television being invisible as it is transmitted through the air may seem strange, but it is actually based on the science of vibration. This vibration, which is present in the form of a magnetic field, can be divided into a virtually limitless number of separate emanations. In this way, if we had a thousand different channels, the magnetic field could be differentiated amongst them. This phenomenon is a fascinating example of the complexity of the science of vibrations.

We have come to understand that vibration in a magnetic field can be divided into an infinite complexity of separate emanations. This means that if we were to have a thousand different channels, we could differentiate them in the magnetic fields so that each one could be broadcast correctly. This realization helps us to understand that there is something out there that is being transmitted in this way. We are able to comprehend the power and significance of this form of transmission and its implications.

In addition to air, helium, and oxygen, there are many other factors that we take into consideration when studying the natural world. Most of these factors have been given scientific explanations, but there is something else that we cannot easily explain or measure. It is an elusive and mysterious force that pervades all of life. We are in the presence of something that connects us to the greater world around us. It is a force of nature that we can feel but cannot see. It is something that binds us to the Earth and creates a sense of interrelatedness between all living things. We are part of a larger whole, part of a greater universal force that is beyond our comprehension. This mysterious agent is part of everything that we are and it is essential to our understanding of the natural world.

Studying the effects of magnetism on the human body, we learn that each individual is surrounded by a unique etheric energy field. This field is also known as an aura, but it is not the same aura that is referred to in metaphysics. This magnetic field is an area of energy that is distinct and unique to each person. This energy field is a powerful force and has the potential to influence and shape our lives. It is essential that we recognize the importance of this energy field and the impact it can have on our lives. We must be mindful of how we interact with this energy and strive to use it to our advantage. By understanding the power of magnetism and its influence on the human body, we can begin to unlock the secrets of our unique aura and use it to help us lead a more balanced and harmonious life.

The energy field which surrounds our physical bodies is a powerful and protective force that extends from three to five feet in all directions. This egg-like atmosphere is known as the energy field, and it is the foundation of all virtue. Our energy field has the ability to affect our moods, emotions, thoughts, and the attitudes of those around us. It is essential to maintain a healthy energy field in order to remain healthy and strong. By taking care of our bodies, we can ensure that our energy fields are strong and capable of protecting us from all negative influences. Additionally, it is important to be mindful of the energy we are sending out into the world. If we can take control of our energy fields, we can make sure that we are sending out positive vibes that will attract positivity and harmony in our lives.

If an individual is able to maintain a healthy balance between their mental, emotional, and physical states, it forms a magnetic field of protection. This protection is normal, healthy, and capable of handling infections and all kinds of difficulties. The protection will help to heal wounds, recover the use of functions, organs, and even compensate for a loss of a certain part. In other words, it is able to provide the body with the strength and resilience to face any challenge.

If we are deprived of a certain body part, it can be compensated for as long as we take proper care of our magnetic field. Our magnetic field is an important part of our well-being, and when we take care of it, it will serve us. The magnetic field is a subtle energy field that contains information about our body, mind, and spirit. It is an energetic field that extends beyond our physical body and is affected by our thoughts, emotions, and environment. Taking proper care of our magnetic field involves being mindful of our thoughts, feelings, and actions. It also means being aware of the environment around us and how it is affecting our energy. Taking time to meditate, practice mindful breathing, and be mindful of our diet and lifestyle can all have a positive impact on our magnetic field. When we are mindful of our magnetic field, we are able to experience greater physical, mental, and spiritual health.

The magnetic field is an important part of our lives and morality that is often overlooked. We tend to not pay much attention to it, but the reality is that our very survival depends on it. The integrity of the magnetic field is dependent on the flow of energy that comes from the sun. Without this flow of energy, it would be impossible for us to exist. This energy is what allows us to keep living and surviving. It is essential for us to recognize the importance of the magnetic field and to take steps to ensure its continued integrity for our own benefit.

This energy comes from the sun, a mysterious energy that travels through the magnetic field, directly entering us through the top of the head. This energy then spreads throughout our bodies, leaving through the lower centres of the body. It is then re-cleansed by solar energy, creating a small, private tank of life that we all carry with us at all times. This tank of life is constantly being replenished and energized by the sun, allowing us to live our lives with vigour and vitality.

Morality is something we must take seriously, as when we break rules, we damage the natural flow of life. We must adhere to the laws of nature and, ultimately, of God or the Source, as their violation can lead to the weakening of the magnetic field. This weakening can be caused by physical interferences, as well as by excessive and wasteful living. We must be conscious of our actions, as they can have lasting effects on the magnetic field and, consequently, our lives.

When this vital field of health is damaged, it has an immediate effect on an individual's vitality. This damage makes the individual more vulnerable to contagious diseases and infections, and overall, it drastically reduces their life expectancy. It is therefore essential to preserve good health in order to live a longer and healthier life.

The Ancients believed that morality was rooted in obedience to the word of God, and in more modern times, it is understood as obedience to the evident will of God as it is revealed in creation. Thus, virtue is that which upholds and strengthens the natural order of the universe, while vice is that which destroys and weakens it. This is the soul of morality, the foundation upon which all other moral considerations are based. For the Ancients, such morality was seen as a divinely ordained law; for modern people, it is an ethical system rooted in natural law and the will of God.

We are good not because the book says we should be nor because it was funded by the laws on Sinai. Rather, we are good because we keep the rules of the integration of the human structure, using the magnetic fields correctly, thereby protecting our health, happiness, and well-being. This is why we should continue to adhere to the rules and regulations put in place for our benefit.

The body as a whole has a magnetic field surrounding it as Kilna demonstrates in his work on the human atmosphere. This same field can be seen in his study of the atom. But this is only a phase of the whole. Each part of the body has its own magnetic field and its own unit of energy. This energy is present in the tiniest subdivision of the individual. It is this energy that allows for the survival of each unit within the individual.

The concept of a "dead particle" in the universe is a paradox. On one hand, the act of killing a particle is seen as the extinguishing of life, however, on the other hand, the very act of disintegration is a symbol of life energy. This leads us to the realization that we must abide by the laws of energy in order to maintain virtue. The energy field is a constant source of life, and as such, we must strive to protect it and ensure its continuity. The universe is an ever-changing ecosystem, and understanding the laws of energy is essential for us to live in harmony with it. The laws of energy are not static, but instead, can be adjusted and adapted to suit our needs. Ultimately, energy laws are a powerful tool to maintain virtue and ensure our collective well-being.

The law of the energy field is a powerful force that governs our lives in ways we may not even be aware of. This law is often referred to as the law of integrity and is based on the idea that we create our own reality based on our thoughts and actions. This law states that when we act with integrity and make decisions that are right for us, we are rewarded with positive energy. Conversely, when we make decisions that are wrong for us, we experience negative energy.

The energy TPL – Technology Performance Level - tells us that to lose our disposition and the temporary fit is wrong to do so. Negative attitudes, such as compromising the principles of right living, thinking badly, and feeling unpleasant, can have a damaging effect on our magnetic field. Consequently, it is important to act in ways that are beneficial to the common good, to ensure that we are not damaging our magnetic field. Engaging in activities and concepts that go against the common good can have a detrimental effect on our energy field, and should be avoided. By taking the appropriate steps to protect our magnetic field, we can ensure that we maintain a healthy energy balance and maximize our potential.

The stomach, as part of the human body, is not just an organ, but a living organism. It is composed of many different parts, all of which are linked to one another in some way. Not only does the stomach have a magnetic field, but so does the heart, brain, glandular structure, intestines, motor system, nervous system, and endocrine system. All of these organs and systems have their own magnetic fields and are interconnected in ways that are still being studied. This interconnectedness allows for a variety of different functions and capabilities within the body, each of which is essential in maintaining health. The complexity of this system is one of the many reasons why the human body is so amazing.

Organs are essential components of living organisms. They work together harmoniously, acting like cogs in a machine, to keep the organism functioning properly. Without all of them working together in unison, the organism would suffer. To harm one organ is to damage all, and to neglect one is to neglect them all. Each organ has its own specific role in the body, and it is only when all of these roles are fulfilled that the grand magnetic field of the person is complete. This field is like a shield of protection, keeping the person healthy and functioning. Without it, the person would be vulnerable to a variety of ailments and ailments and would ultimately fail to thrive.

Going back to the ancient Greek philosopher Pythagoras, we can understand the concept of therapy being a result of the contemplation of symmetrical geometric solids. In ancient Egypt, there was a temple dedicated to this practice, with images of mathematical cubes and octagons placed upon a pedestal for contemplation. This was a way of bringing people together and relieving stress, as the contemplation of these shapes was thought to be calming. Through this process, people could use geometrical shapes to bring a sense of balance and harmony to their lives. This practice is still used today, as people often find solace in the contemplation of shapes and patterns.

We must look upon the energy of the Stone solids as a reality in our lives now. These Stone solids may have appeared to be inert and without life, but in reality, they were very much alive. Every form in nature, natural or artificial, has a magnetic field, from the smallest atom to the largest galaxy. The magnetic fields are present and the rules of each of them need to be obeyed. This applies to the Stone solids as well, which have their own unique magnetic fields that we must take into consideration. By acknowledging the energy of the Stone solids and understanding their magnetic fields, we can continue to progress and thrive in our lives.

When an individual looks at a geometric solid and perceives perfect proportions, the imagery of that solid is sent into their consciousness in the form of a benevolent magnetic center. This means that the individual is seeing harmony and perceiving something in perfect order and correctness. The sight of perfection has the power to improve or harmonize any discord that may exist. This realization can have a profound effect on the subconscious life of the individual, as it brings about a sense of balance and order.

Everywhere we look in nature, we see the benevolence of its creations. It is only when these gifts are abused, mostly by humanity, that these natural blessings are lost. We live in a world that has become increasingly corrupt, and this can be overwhelming and intimidating. We can become so scared or overwhelmed that we choose to take the path of least resistance and follow along with everyone else. However, we must remember that we can still make a change, and strive to restore the benevolence of nature. If we work together, we can make a difference and bring back the natural beauty and kindness that once existed.

It isn't really the way it was intended to be, the bad news that we have has nothing to do with us unless we are part of the bad program. You might say it's nicer to imagine a world in which we could all work together, and there's no doubt about it that things would be much better. Until such time as that happens, however, the individual who is trying to do right has to be careful not to be infected by a common disillusionment. It's a difficult situation we are in, and it can be hard to stay positive when faced with such news. But staying strong and having faith that things will get better can help us find our way back to a better future.

Individuals must be mindful of the basic values they hold true and the energy resources they use to protect them. It is possible for one person to make a difference in the world, so it is important for those individuals to preserve their resources so that they can be available to help bring about positive change. Despite the challenges and trials that life may bring, one should never become so discouraged that they forget the importance of their own resources and the potential impact they can have. By holding on to this truth, individuals can keep their hope alive that they can help to shape history.

Disillusionment, despair, discouragement, bitterness, anger, and frustration are all powerful emotions that can have a huge impact on us. While their effects may be directed outwardly, they ultimately affect the individual who uses them. Instead of allowing these emotions to take control of our lives, we should try to find ways to better understand them and use them in a constructive manner. Through this understanding, we can make more positive choices that will lead to healthier, more fulfilling lives. It is important to remember that these emotions do not have to be negative, but can be used as a source of motivation and growth. By taking the time to understand and use these emotions constructively, we can truly transform our lives.

No matter what we read in the paper or hear on the radio or television, we must remember that there is a greater good at work in our lives. This great good is a magnetic force that extends throughout our solar system and even beyond, into the entire galaxy. It is this magnetic field that holds within itself the power to make all things good, and to ultimately succeed. We must remember this, no matter the situation or challenge we face. The great good will always prevail in the end.

We must all understand that we cannot achieve success if we do not put in the effort. We must strive to make sure our actions are of the utmost quality, regardless of the outcome. We must recognize that our values and morals remain constant, regardless of the decisions and actions of those around us. We will never be punished for the mistakes of others, nor rewarded for the accomplishments of others. In the end, it is up to us to make sure we are putting forth our best effort, and that we are not relying on the achievements of others to achieve success.

We must achieve these things ourselves through our own efforts, our own integrities, and our own dedication. All of this is added up in a mysterious bank account, which is called energy or magnetic resource. It is there to serve us, to provide us with the ability to succeed and flourish. However, if an individual does wrong, the service collapses and the individual who does wrong eventually finds themselves without the resources they need to advance. Therefore, it is essential that we act in a way that serves ourselves and others. By doing this, we ensure that the resources in this mysterious bank account remain available to us so that we can achieve our goals and fulfil our potential.

The Centre of Consciousness is a part of ourselves that we must strive to keep in a state of correctness. In Buddhism, this is referred to as the Saptaparna or the house or temple with seven rooms. It is within this temple that the individual has to take the great initiation against the hindrances. This initiation begins with recognizing our own inner strength and accepting our own integrity as our own source of strength. We must learn to trust in this strength and to rely on it in times of difficulty. Only when we have mastered this process can we begin to move forward and make positive changes in our lives.

The realization of the immutability of good and the inevitability of right or wrong is something deeply embedded in the heart of every honest person. It is a truth that leads to inner peace, a peace that can only be found in the quiet and tranquil dunes of life.

The endless and continuous process of redemption is seen everywhere in nature. All things, in due time, will come back to the peace which they sacrificed for. This truth is absolute, and it is a truth that can help lead us to a wave of deep inner peace.

No matter the hardships or trials we face in life, it is important to remember that redemption is possible. The realization of the immutability of good and the inevitability of right or wrong is something that can help us find peace and tranquillity in chaos.

As individuals, we sometimes forget the larger, Universal reality that we are part of. But when we look around us, we are reminded of the incredible beauty of this world that we live in. Unfortunately, our actions are causing us to slowly but surely destroy this world and ourselves. We must take this opportunity to recognize the importance of the Universal reality and take the necessary steps to ensure its preservation. We must remember that we are all connected and that our choices have an impact not only on us but also on the world around us. By understanding our place in this larger reality, we can start to make better, more sustainable decisions that will ultimately benefit us all.

It is not some vast cosmic power that compels us to be selfish and prioritize profit over principle;

these concepts do not exist in nature. We know that with moderation, integrity, and dedication, we could all live in peace, and even accommodate another five billion people. Unfortunately, we are sacrificing so much to obtain short-term gains and, if we continue to act this way, our energy resources will be depleted. We must strive to be mindful and responsible in our actions so that we can ensure a sustainable and prosperous future for all.

We are deeply concerned about the changes taking place in our atmosphere and the toll that our over-reliance on natural resources is having on our environment. We cannot keep wasting the magnetic field of the human body or the planet's magnetic field, or else we will suffer the consequences. Just as we are running out of petroleum, we are also running out of the ability to regenerate our resources. We must find ways to be more sustainable if we are to keep our planet safe and prosperous.

If we recklessly dispose of and waste our recuperative power, the magnetism that helps our digestion can be destroyed. Our bodies are built on a delicate balance of energy and forces that must be maintained in order to remain healthy and functional. Our digestive system relies on the magnetic forces that are generated by recuperative power to help break down and absorb the nutrients needed to survive. When these forces are disrupted by the careless disposal of our recuperative power, it can cause serious digestive issues that can lead to more serious health problems. Therefore, it is important to be mindful of how we use our recuperative power and to try to minimize its waste. By doing so, we can help to protect the magnetism that is essential for proper digestion.

Corruption can be dangerous not just in the world at large, but also in our own lives. When we consume unhealthy foods, adopt unhealthy attitudes, or make decisions in a negative frame of mind, we put ourselves at risk. The same can be said of the world at large; when we make decisions and act in a way that is not beneficial to ourselves or to the planet, we endanger our own existence. As an ancient Indian saying goes, "The great mother of the Earth has cast many civilizations from her back." Let us take care not to be the next one.

Everything that goes beyond a certain point is destroyed because it disrupts its connection with its source of energy. Without its main source of energy, magnetism, it can no longer sustain itself. Magnetism is found in the food that nourishes us, in the air we breathe, in the earth that grows our vegetables, and in our own souls. It is the magnetism that helps us to hope for the good things in life, even if we are not able to achieve them. Although destruction is inevitable, we must remember that magnetism is the ultimate source of sustenance - it is what keeps us alive.

We go on year after year making all kinds of efforts to feel better, be better and think better but often overlook the fact that all of these things depend upon the life-giving force of the Earth itself.

If we destroy or abuse this resource, the Earth will become ever more sterile and the air will become increasingly polluted. We must do all we can to protect this vital energy resource and ensure that our planet remains healthy and vibrant for future generations.

The concept of religion is simple yet profound – it is the proper use of the resources we have been given for the greater good of all. It is about using our privileges not for ourselves, but for the betterment of the world and its people. Religion is not only about having faith and following the teachings of a higher power but also about recognizing the importance of charity and compassion towards others. This concept has been around for centuries and is still relevant today. Knowing that we have a responsibility to be good stewards of the world, and to use our resources in a way that benefits humanity, is an essential part of being a person of faith. By living this concept, we can make a difference in the lives of others and create a more peaceful and prosperous society.

We have been given the opportunity to create something beautiful with the gardeners we have added to the garden. We have been given a beautiful planet, and have chosen to subdivide and sell it for profits. Yet, we have forgotten the original purpose – that we should come together as one, working together for the betterment of each other and the glory of the universe. It is time that we take back our planet and focus on the greater good. By working together, we can create something even more beautiful and beneficial for all. We can create a world that values the environment and the people who inhabit it. Let us begin this journey together, and make the world a better place for everyone.

We are being prepared for a bigger job than we are currently undertaking, and it is important to note that our current failure in the examination is not indicative of our future potential. Everything we do should be measured by the potential profit it could bring, but we must also remember that freedom from responsibility is equally important. We must be responsible with our energy, or else it will be wasted forever. By the time we reach forever, we must have made the most of our energy and the opportunities it has provided us.

We have been given an incredible gift - a beautiful garden to tend to and care for, as the Muslim faith calls it, the Garden of Allah. Unfortunately, we have neglected our duties as keepers and gardeners, allowing the garden to succumb to weeds and disrepair. We have the power to use the resources of the Earth for good, to build and create and bring about peace and understanding. Instead, we dig deep and create materials that bring about war, death, and destruction. This is a lesson in morality, that we must use the power we have been given wisely so that our garden can remain beautiful and peaceful.

All these things are little things but they all add up to the loss and waste of magnetic resources they are the failure of the individual

to protect the source of his own life, the source of his own future and the

breaking of the laws and rules by which he must compare his own needs with the needs of others,

The little choices we make every day may seem insignificant, but they all add up to the waste of precious resources. When we fail to take care of our natural environment, we are not only endangering our own lives and future but also the lives and futures of others. We must be mindful of our actions and consider how our needs compare to those of others. We must strive to maintain a balance between our own needs and the needs of those around us. By doing so, we can ensure that our environment and its resources are preserved for generations to come.

It is essential that we recognize the importance of protecting the Toadstool, as well as the nation if we are to achieve lasting peace. We must protect the small things because each of them is an important energy resource. Unfortunately, it is often our viewpoint that the small should be controlled by the big, such that the small and humble are left to be exploited. This is an unacceptable truth and must not be tolerated. We must strive to ensure that everyone has the right to be respected and protected, regardless of their size. Only then can we truly have world peace.

Everything in life is meant to be utilized, not abused. When someone abuses any part of life, they are actually contributing to the destruction. That said, the world we live in is filled with forces that seek to cooperate and work together for the greater good. It is our responsibility to make the best of these forces, rather than using them for our own selfish purposes. We must play games that are constructive, rather than seeking to conquer everything with our own selfish desires. By doing so, we can ensure a brighter future for all.

Putting something in orbit is just the beginning of what we are trying to accomplish. Our true goal is to understand how to conquer, win, and achieve our aspirations. We can do this by putting ourselves in orbit and abiding by the rules of the game of Life: serving it as it should be served and loving it as it should be loved. We can do this by understanding the importance of these two steps and acting on them. Only then can we truly conquer, win, and achieve our goals.

We should strive to admire the good and protect it, allowing it to slowly and quietly outgrow anything that is of lesser quality. If we can do this, these resources and magnetic fields can supply us with enough energy to power the world for millions of years. This is a remarkable prospect that should inspire us to do our best to use these resources responsibly. With the right knowledge and respect for the environment, we can create a future that is both sustainable and bright.

2

Chapter Two

Sacred Geometry

"Geometry is the knowledge that appears to be produced by human beings, yet whose meaning is totally independent of them"

- Rudolf Steiner-

The mysterious background net of the master designers of Ancient Egypt has never been made public. It is believed that the net was not just used to arrange the aspects of art on temple walls, but it had a vibrational component as well. This ancient knowledge has been passed down to modern times and is now used in Egyptian bio-geometry. By using this ancient technique, we are able to test the vibrational qualities of any person or place. This mysterious background net of the master designers of Ancient Egypt has been kept alive and is still used to this day.

The ancient Egyptians were well known for their understanding of bio-geometry. It was a way to measure and understand the vibrational qualities of any person, place, or thing. This knowledge was passed down through many traditions, including the

Himalayan tradition of Shakti. This unique concept was the carrier wave that sent all the other energies. It is a powerful way to explore the depths of the energetic field and gain a better understanding of the relationship between the person and their environment. By studying bio-geometry, we can gain a greater awareness of the subtle vibrations that permeate our world and how they are affecting us. By learning to tap into this energy, we can explore the mysteries of the universe and gain a deeper understanding of our place in it.

The French were fascinated by the discovery of wave energy that could penetrate thicknesses of lead that could not be penetrated by X-rays. This wave energy, known as the negative green carrier wave energy, is responsible for moving energy from one location to another in the physical body, which makes the organs work. Additionally, it sends things from one system to another, allowing for more efficient functioning of the body. This wave energy is a revolutionary discovery and its potential uses are vast.

It is what conducts the energy of the body and is what allows us to experience a deep level of sexual energy and vitality. This energy is conducted through the energy meridians of the body, most notably the acupuncture meridians from Chinese tradition. This energy is the foundation for emotional, mental, and physical health, as it breaks down resistance in the mind and body and opens them up to positive shifts in our lives. By tapping into this energy, we can become aware of any subconscious blockages that may be preventing us from growth, and move through them with ease. This energy is the key to unlocking our full potential and achieving lasting well-being.

At the spiritual level, it is the act of blessing, prayer, and meditation that conducts the energy from higher plane levels into the human physical body. The more spiritual activities a person does, the stronger the vibration is from their energetic field. All of our modern technology is based on cracking two codes – the code of matter and the code of energy. The code of matter deals with physical matter, while the code of energy is related to the spiritual and energetic realm. As the spiritual practices of blessing, prayer, and meditation increase, the vibration of the energetic field also increases, allowing for more energy to be conducted into the physical body. This energy is then used by the body to fuel its physical, mental, and spiritual activities.

The spectrum of electromagnetic energy and physical matter are two distinct yet interconnected phenomena. The code of the spectrum of electromagnetic energy is the set of rules that govern the behavior of light and other forms of electromagnetic radiation. This spectrum is composed of radio waves, microwaves, infrared radiation, visible light, ultraviolet radiation, x-rays, and gamma rays. The code of the spectrum of physical matter is the set of rules that govern the behavior of atoms, molecules, and other forms of matter. This spectrum is composed of solids, liquids, and gases. Both the electromagnetic spectrum and the physical matter spectrum are essential to understanding the world around us.

In the late 1800s, Dmitri Mendeleev in Russia cracked the code when he developed the periodic table of elements, a spectrum of physical matter. By understanding the exact elements and their electromagnetic energy, scientists were able to put the two together and create the technology of today. The periodic table of elements is the basis of modern technology and has thus been a major contributor to the progress of our world. Its importance has only increased over time, and the discoveries made by Mendeleev are still the foundation of our understanding of the physical world.

The car's ability to run is based on a combination of two things: mechanics and energy. However, as bio-geometry has often explained, there is more to the equation than this. Every classical tradition focused on the level of vital life force, something that modern science and medicine have overlooked in the last couple of hundred years. This life force, or energy, is essential to the functioning of the car, as it is what powers the mechanics. Without it, the car would not be able to run. Therefore, it is essential to recognize both the mechanics and the life force as integral components of a running car.

Our understanding of the world has been greatly enhanced by the study of vital life forces and higher consciousness. These aspects of existence exist beyond the physical and can be manipulated to achieve outcomes on the physical plane. It is believed that these powers actually work at the causative level, which is the level that gives rise to the physical plane. Thus, we can assume that the manipulation of vital life forces and higher consciousness could have an effect on the physical plane. By understanding these forces and how they interact, we can gain greater control of our lives and the events that occur around us.

Rudolf Steiner's solution to the confusion between the physical and the electromagnetic was to recognize the vital life force, which is the foundation of every scientific and healing system, as a level above and distinct from both the physical and the electromagnetic. This life force is the foundation of our physical and spiritual existence, and it is the bridge between the two. It is the energy that flows within and around us, as well as between us and the Universe. Steiner's approach emphasized the importance of developing an understanding of the life force and how to use it to improve our lives, health, and spiritual development. He believed that the vital life force is the source of our physical and spiritual well-being and that it can be manipulated to bring about positive changes. By understanding and utilizing the vital life force, we can make a profound difference in our lives, both physically and spiritually.

The human body is composed of a complex network of cells, organs, and systems, each of which are designed to perform a specific task. However, this intricate system would be nothing more than an inert mass of molecules without the life-giving energy of these higher vibrational levels. This energy is believed to help animate physical substances and bring the seemingly-inanimate physical body to life.

These higher energies are said to be in a constant state of vibration, permeating the physical and metaphysical realms alike. They are believed to give life to the physical and to provide a conduit through which spiritual energies can flow. This energy is essential to the functioning of the human body and is a vital part of maintaining health and balance.

In conclusion, the concept of scalar waves and higher energies from the vibrational level is an integral part of many ancient cultures and traditions. These energies are believed to penetrate down into the physical realm and animate physical substances, such as the human body. This energy is essential to the functioning of the human body and is a vital part of maintaining health and balance.

Without this energy, physical substances would become a corpse and slowly begin to disintegrate. This process is known as Hertzian waves, as described by Tesla, and results in an electromagnetic spectrum. This poses a problem, as there is a new technology that is highly efficient at manipulating physical structures but fails to consider the effect of vibration. This could potentially lead to disastrous results if the vibration is not considered. To ensure that this does not happen, it is essential to consider the effect of vibration when utilizing this technology.

Modern biology has been stripped of its living aspect, leaving many feelings disconnected from the life force that has been known and understood for thousands of years. People who attempt to talk about life force in modern biology are often labelled as victims of the vitalism fallacy and are dismissed by the scientific community. This has resulted in the knowledge and techniques of ancient healing practices such as Ayurveda and Mayan healing being cast aside and forgotten. However, there is a growing trend of people seeking out these ancient practices in order to better understand and nurture the life force within themselves and the world around them. This is a positive sign, showing that the ancient wisdom of our ancestors is still relevant today and that there is much to be gained from it.

The French have identified the vibrational spectrum, which is inextricably connected to the vital life force itself, as a key component of modern bio-geometry. This knowledge is rooted in ancient

Egypt, though it is presented in a new and modern form. By identifying the electromagnetic and physical spectrums, the French have been able to uncover the importance of the vibrational spectrum to modern bio-geometry. This knowledge has enabled them to make significant advances in bio-geometry and has become the foundation for its modern iteration.

Dr. Ibrahim Karim's discoveries have been ground-breaking for the field of biology. He was able to demonstrate that by applying simple geometric forms to biological life, he could change the life functions of a biological system. In particular, he identified the French vibrational spectrum of 12 bands, each of which has a very particular power. This power is a polarization power, which has the potential to dramatically alter biological life. Dr. Karim's discoveries have been incredibly influential and have opened up a whole new realm of possibilities for researchers. His discoveries have demonstrated that even a small geometric form can have a large impact on biological life.

Dr. Karim spoke of a power that transcends the concept of duality - the power of singularity and of the original center. He said that some energies are more Yin, some are more Yang, some are activating, and some are more sedating, but that there is a greater power that lies beyond polarity. That power is the energy of the unified source of all creation - a power that is beyond the idea of duality where everything is one. This power is the original source of all creation, the source of all life and energy, and it is a power that is beyond all understanding.

Dr. Karim then began to apply these vibrational methods that the French had pioneered in modern times based on their inspiration from ancient Egypt. He was able to identify the vibrational characteristics of that energy of the center of that original unified source, the energy that harmonizes and balances all living energy systems. He discovered a way to do this not through applying an opposite polarity for polarity balance, but instead through vibrational technology. This technology allowed him to detect the exact energy signatures of the energy center in order to bring balance and harmony. He was able to identify how to precisely apply the energy techniques developed by the ancient Egyptians to both living and non-living systems. His discoveries opened up a whole new world of vibrational energy that has been invaluable to the world of healing and energy science.

Dr Karim's research found that the center of the vibration is characterized by a golden vibration, which is a concept shared by various classical traditions. According to these traditions, the golden vibration is believed to be the source of physical gold, which is essentially the crystallization of a subtler vibration from a higher plane into the physical plane. This notion is found in many different traditions, from the Dallas to the Christians.

The ancient Egyptians were quite literal when they talked about gold, as they understood that gold was a representation of the highest spiritual energy. When a person advances spiritually, they develop a golden aura around their head and body as they are in resonance with the original unified source. This understanding was further explored by Dr. Karim, who was able to identify some of the secrets of ancient Egypt through bio-geomancy. He was able to see and understand the power of the spiritual connection between gold and the higher source. Through his work, he was able to see how gold could be used to help people to spiritually ascend and gain wisdom. He also was able to gain insight into the power of gold to help people to connect to the divine source. Dr. Karim's work was a revolutionary discovery that helped to explain the spiritual significance of gold and its role in ancient Egypt.

The concept of different geometric forms resonating with different levels of creation, or what Dr. Karim calls planes of nature, is the basis of the advanced level of bio-geometry developed by Ibrahim Karim. This level is known as the Ibrahim Karim Universal Pendulum. This pendulum is shaped based on the waveforms created by the geometric forms, and these waveforms are said to create various energetic effects. Furthermore, it is thought that these geometric forms interact with different planes of nature, thus allowing for a deeper level of understanding of our world. By tapping into these planes of nature, we can begin to understand the deeper meaning and significance behind the shapes, forms, and energetic effects created by the different geometric forms. This understanding can then be used to create therapeutic and healing effects.

The physical, vital, emotional, astral, mental, causal, spiritual, and divine levels all have particular geometries that resonate with them. By using the correct geometric form, a person can tap into the power of each of these planes. It is believed that each one of these planes can offer unique benefits and opportunities when accessed. By combining the geometries of each of these planes, a person can create a powerful, synergistic structure that amplifies the effects of each plane. Ultimately, this structure can be used to access higher levels of consciousness, achieve personal growth, and unlock a person's higher potential.

The ancient Egyptians were masters of sacred geometry and understood the power it has to connect them to higher planes. By utilizing this knowledge, they were able to create an antenna-like device out of various shapes and symbols that allowed them to access and resonate with higher planes. This device was known as a resonance antenna and was used to communicate with their gods and deities. The Egyptians believed that through this direct resonant exchange, they could access divine power and knowledge from the higher planes. This resonant antenna has become an essential part of many spiritual practices throughout history, as it has the potential to open people to a higher level of consciousness and understanding.

The astral plane, or the emotional body, is an outer plane in the Western tradition, which is referred to as a source of light. This plane is connected to the form of a hemisphere or a pyramid, and when this form is used it is not just for its power, but also to represent the connection to the astral plane. This plane is believed to be a realm where emotions, desires, and thoughts are expressed and explored. It is believed to be the home of consciousness, and the place where we feel and experience our connection to the universe. Through this connection, we can understand and explore our feelings, desires, and thoughts, which can help us to gain clarity and insight into our lives. Thus, the astral plane can be seen as a kind of inner sanctuary, where we can find balance, peace, and insight.

Pyramid power is an energy that is believed to be derived from the shape of the pyramid itself. It was first identified by the French as a negative green ray, or "penetrating carrier ray," that is emitted from both the hemisphere and pyramid shapes. This ray is believed to be an antenna to the astral plane, enabling the pyramid to “capture” this power. It is believed that the pyramid shape is what allows it to capture this power because the angles of the pyramid shape are thought to create a sort of "vacuum" that can hold this energy. This energy has been used for many different purposes, from healing and protection to energy transmission. While there is still much to be discovered about pyramid power, it is a fascinating concept that has been used for centuries.

By making a slight indentation in the center of the four faces of the pyramid, the shape of the pyramid was modified. This indentation is so subtle that it cannot be seen from the ground, and can only be viewed from the air. From the air, the slight indentation of the faces of the major pyramids at the Giza plateau can be clearly seen. This slight modification changed the resonance of the pyramid from the general astral plane. It is believed that this modification gave the pyramid an enhanced spiritual power, allowing it to become a powerful spiritual symbol.

The lower astral has some questionable energetics that can be difficult to resonate with the higher astral. However, when we use the power of the pyramid, this energy can be cleansed and balanced. The pyramid is a powerful tool that has been used for centuries to help bring balance to areas of chaos and imbalance, and this is no different. By using the pyramid's energy, we can help to bridge the gap between the lower and higher astral realms, creating a harmonious and more balanced environment. This can be quite beneficial for those who are stuck in stagnant energy and need a little extra help to move forward. By focusing on the power of the pyramid, we can transform the energy of the lower astral into something that is more productive and beneficial for all.

The ancient civilizations were aware of the power of geometry and the ability it had to act as an antenna to connect with higher planes of creation. This connection would then cause a specific vibration to be emitted through the shape-caused wave. This vibration was so powerful that the ancients were able to not only work with the general negative green ray but also delve into the sub-bands. This secret knowledge of the power of geometry and its ability to resonate on a higher plane has been lost to the ages but remains an incredibly powerful and useful tool.

The placement of the King's Chamber inside the Great Pyramid is not in the exact middle, as one might expect. Instead, it is located 6 degrees 15 minutes off the center. This placement was done to get a particular carrier wave within the negative green band, a sweet spot in the entire band. This spot allows a person to connect to higher dimensional levels through a carrier wave.

We can explore a bit more about how vertical and horizontal wave pendulums work for each of the bands. When the energy is propagated parallel to the earth's surface, it is called a horizontal wave. On the other hand, when the energy moves perpendicular to the surface, it is known as a vertical wave. Understanding these two different types of waves is essential to comprehending how they interact with each other, and how they affect our environment.

The power of waves can create different biological effects, which is why it is important to be able to detect them. We have two different pendulums, both of which are fairly simple to use. Not only can they be used for designing things that have strong vibrations to them, but they can also be used to test things that naturally have this energy. What makes a spiritual power spot in nature is that it has a strong concentration of BG3 waves. With the use of pendulums, it is possible to detect, analyze and measure the concentration of BG3 waves in a specific area. This can be incredibly useful for detecting and understanding the spiritual power spots in nature.

Classical traditions are guardians of specific places on the Earth's surface that are imbued with spiritual power. These places, known as power spots, can be identified by their strong concentration of BG3 vibration. This vibration is a force that can be felt and experienced, and it is a sure sign of a true power spot. False power spots are those locations that have been falsely claimed to be power spots, lacking the BG3 vibration. It is important that we differentiate between the two so that we can be sure to experience the full spiritual power of a true power spot.

The speed g3 energy functions in two distinct ways: it energizes and strengthens the body's existing energy, and it helps to create new energy pathways. This energy helps to strengthen the body's existing energy, which allows it to better heal itself, and it helps to create new energy pathways, which can be especially useful for healing and restoring balance.

This energy also helps to increase the flow of energy throughout the body. It helps to open up energy blocks and clear stagnant energy, allowing the body to better heal itself. Additionally, this energy helps to restore balance in the body's energy system. It helps to balance out excess energy, allowing the body to function at its peak efficiency.

The microcosm of the human body is home to a variety of powerful spots, such as the chakras, acupuncture points, and cells. These spots all possess the speed g3 energy, which has a range of energetic functions. This energy is capable of strengthening the energetic pathways in the body, creating a clearer connection between the physical and spiritual realms. It can also be used to heal and restore balance to the body and mind. Additionally, this energy can be used to promote a sense of grounding and inner peace. It can be used to attract positive energy and to ward off negative or harmful energies. Ultimately, the speed g3 energy is an invaluable source of well-being, capable of helping to provide balance, harmony, and healing to the body.

The speed g3 energy is an incredibly powerful healing tool, and it can be used in a variety of ways. It can be used to help with healing physical ailments, as well as emotional and spiritual issues. Ultimately, the speed of g3 energy is incredibly

In ancient Egypt, the mysteries of the heart were known, and their understanding of the heart's importance extended beyond the physical level and into the realm of consciousness. The sinoatrial node, or sinus node, which is the master pacemaker of the body, was understood to be the place where the heart's vital energy was concentrated. It was believed that this energy had a profound impact on human consciousness and that it could be used to unlock mysteries of the heart. Thus, the ancient Egyptians used their knowledge of the heart's biosignature to unlock the mysteries of the heart and to gain a deeper understanding of its power and importance.

The ancient Egyptians believed in a spiritual realm that was higher than our physical world and they believed that this spiritual realm could be accessed through Sufi traditions. Even today, Sufi traditions are still practiced and believed in, with many people believing that they are a way to restore our connection to higher sources. It is believed that these higher sources resonate in the physical body and that by engaging in Sufi traditions we can access them and gain a greater understanding and connection to spiritual forces. This understanding and connection can help us gain knowledge, insight, and wisdom, and can also help us to open up to a greater sense of peace and harmony. By engaging in Sufi traditions, we can access the higher vibrational forces that can help us to bridge the gap between the physical and spiritual realms, and restore our connection to higher sources.

When we alter the numerical sequence of patterns, it has a profound effect on the vibrational level of the pattern. The numerical sequence is responsible for the vibrational frequency of the pattern, as each number holds a unique frequency. This is why when you change the numerical sequence of the patterns, it changes the level of vibration that the pattern is emitting. Different numerical sequences produce different vibrations, and different vibrations create different outcomes. This is why it is so important to understand the power of numerical sequencing when it comes to pattern creation.

Dr. Karim's project in Switzerland in 2003 proved that electromagnetic fields could be harmonized on a large scale. The project used a variety of tools to create energetic effects in a bio-geometry cube, which was found to concentrate a strong force of BG3 harmonization in the environment. The Hamburg emitter was used as a key component of this project, helping to create the desired results of harmonization. It was a pioneering moment for bio-geometry, laying the groundwork for further exploration into the effects of this type of energy. It was a major milestone in the understanding of how to utilize bio-geometry to harmonize electromagnetic fields.

Dr. Karim's Swiss Project has been one of the most fascinating experiments conducted to date. One aspect of the project focuses on the concept of balancing the brain hemispheres through a toroidal flow of energy. This toroidal flow of energy works by having the energy circulate in a circular motion that can be likened to a ring. This energy flow is believed to be able to provide a powerful balance between the two hemispheres of the brain, allowing the brain to operate more efficiently and with greater harmony. The energy flow is thought to be beneficial in many ways, including improving cognitive abilities and increasing focus. It is also believed to be helpful in reducing stress and anxiety. Dr. Karim's Swiss Project has already seen some amazing results as the toroidal flow of energy has been used to help people with various conditions, including ADHD, autism, and depression. The results have been nothing short of remarkable and many have reported feeling more relaxed and focused after experiencing the toroidal flow of energy. Dr. Karim's Swiss Project is truly a revolutionary experiment and it is exciting to see the potential that the toroidal flow of energy has to offer.

Dr Karim has put forth the concept that in the human energy field, there is a central axis that runs through the body referred to as the spiritual axis. Additionally, there is a time-space axis that runs more on the horizontal axis through the body. These axes play a role in the way energy is expressed and experienced by humans. It is fascinating to explore the ways in which these energies can be manipulated and used for a variety of purposes.

Dr. Karim's lecture revealed a basic idea that when an independent being begins to perceive within space-time, it creates an expansion from the center outward, forming a bulge. Further, when the two forearms are broken apart to form two pillars, a resonance is created. This resonance is thought to be the cause of the bulge.

Dr. Karim refers to them as the pillars of wisdom. The one without the bulge and without the space-time perception resonates strongly with the right brain hemisphere, allowing for an intuitive perception of a human being. The one with the bulge, however, is connected to the space-time perception and the rational faculty of the left brain. This bulge is connected to the center and grounds things into physical reality.

The Duat, or Underworld, is a concept originating from ancient Egyptian tradition. It is said to have many gates one must pass through in order to reach the other side. These gates are part of a toroidal movement, a template that governs the movement of things through space-time and outside of space-time from one dimension to another. This template is said to be the basis of the entire structure of the movement between different worlds, and it is believed to be the perfect expression of the eternal cycle of life and death. By passing through each of the gates, one is able to reach the other side, and thus, the Duat is a representation of the journey through death and rebirth. The concept of the Duat is an important part of the Egyptian religion, and many of the gods and goddesses are associated with the Underworld and its gates. For example, Osiris is said to be the ruler of the Duat, and he is responsible for the souls of the dead when they pass through the gates. The concept of the Duat is still honored today, and it is believed to be an integral part of the cycle of life and death.

It is fascinating to consider that the same pattern is replicated at ever-increasing levels and scales. Whether we look at our own energy fields or great dimensional structures, we can see this same pattern manifesting. It is an incredible reminder of the interconnectedness of all things and of the powerful potential of this pattern to create, heal, and transform. It is a reminder that we are all part of something larger, something infinitely powerful, and something we can access when we are open to its possibilities. Every time we open up to the possibilities of this pattern, we position ourselves to create and experience something new and beautiful

Sacred geometry is a fascinating field of study that seeks to explain the nature of reality. It posits that all things, from the smallest molecule to the largest structures in the universe, are constructed from a set of basic geometric shapes. This idea of scale and variance is key to understanding how our brain, and by extension our ability to perceive the spiritual, is connected to the same structures that exist in other parts of the universe.

It is believed that our brains are capable of resonance, where they are able to pick up on the same frequency of energy that exists beyond our physical realm. This energy is what is thought to be found in various dimensional gates, or portals, that can be used to access other realms and higher levels of understanding. By understanding the scale and variance of sacred geometry, we can gain insight into how our brains are connected to these gates, and how we can use them to grow spiritually and gain access to deeper truths.

The Egyptian Book of the Dead is a collection of ancient Egyptian texts translated into modern times. It is believed that these texts were used as a guide to help people navigate the afterlife, as well as an initiation into being able to travel through the gates. It is an important part of ancient Egyptian culture and is believed to have been inscribed on the walls of the tombs of the deceased. It was not known by the same name in Ancient Egypt, however, its purpose is still relevant today. The Egyptian Book of the Dead contains a wide range of texts, from spells to hymns to prayers, and more. It is a fascinating glimpse into the beliefs and practices of Ancient Egypt and is a must-read for anyone wishing to explore the culture of this ancient civilization.

The Book of Coming Forth by Day, also known by its original Egyptian name, the Book of the Dead, is an ancient text that speaks of the journey of the dead to the afterlife. It talks of the deceased passing through various gates and chambers, each of which grants them a different level of attainment and experience. This journey has been likened to the New Death Experience, which speaks of the deceased traveling through a tunnel. This tunnel is believed to represent the Tau, a symbol of spiritual and physical completeness.

The internal movement of initiation is akin to a bridge, one that connects the right and left brain perceptions of the human mind. This bridge symbolizes the passing from one state to another, and the human brain itself is representative of a higher dimensional structure, a microcosm of sorts. When one reaches the center point of the bridge, the crossing point in the human brain, they will reach the corpus callosum. This is the essence of initiation, and this movement marks the passing from one world to the next.

At the center point of our interaction lies the bg3 energy, which harmonizes both the left and right hemispheres of human existence. It is at this point that we are able to create the physical existence and anchor it in the space-time continuum. This is facilitated by the left-brain perception, which is an extension of the primordial ocean of energy. This energy can be detected in the pulse of time that is present in the human body, and this pulse of time is connected to a higher source. This higher source can be seen as the connection point between the physical and spiritual realms, and it is this connection that allows us to tap into a higher level of consciousness.

The ancient Egyptians believed that the health of an individual was determined by the balance of the time pulse in the heart pacemaker. This was connected to the weighing of the heart, which was done in the Hall of Judgment. It was believed that when the breath of the lungs and the pulse of the heart were in a particular rhythm, the individual was in balance with something at a higher level. However, when this rhythm was disrupted, health problems could arise. This is why it was so important to maintain the balance of the time pulse in the heart pacemaker in order to ensure good health.

Ma'a Ed is more than just a sound--it's a vibration that has the power to harmonize the time pulse within a person's energy field and put them into resonance. Pronouncing it correctly is essential in order to feel the full effect; by simply saying the words, one can create the sound of Ma'a Ed. This sound has the capability to transform the lungs and heart, as it reverberates throughout the entire body. The power of Ma'a Ed lies in its capacity to bring one into resonance and alignment with the energy field.

3

Chapter Three

The Akashic Records: The Book of Life

"The past is whatever the records and the memories agree upon."
· — **George Orwell, 1984 -**

The Supercomputer Of The Universe That Contains Infinite Information:

It is also called "the Book of Life". It is not a book to pick up but a knowledge plan of the past, present, and future and the key to healing. All events, experiences, and insights are recorded, documented, and stored here. It is the memory of the universe. Everything that exists, every human, every flower possesses the Akasha energy. It is the vibratory field of love. The Akashic Chronicle is where everything is stored; what you experienced from your past and also from a previous life.

For centuries, people have believed that their cosmic archives contain information about the history of humanity and our future. According to Carl Jung, it is the collective unconscious; according to Kevin Tedeschi, it is a universal supercomputer that stores all the information about everything that exists; and according to the prophet Edgar Casey, we're dealing with the Akashic Records. Are they really located in some mysterious place in the universe, and do they contain the answers to all of our questions? How can we access them, and can they tell us more about our future?

According to Edgar Casey, the Akashic Records are the supercomputer of the universe that contains all the information about everything that exists. The Akashic Records are a field of energy that holds past, present, and future knowledge of all things, and it materializes everywhere at the same time. Each element within this global field has its own individual energy fields that can interact in numerous ways. Compare the Akashic Records to the Wi-Fi network; we cannot see it, yet we know it is all around us. It is something invisible to the eyes, but if you connect to it, you can get infinite information. And as Nikola Tesla says, "If you want to discover the secrets of the universe, think in terms of energy, frequency, and vibration." The Western religious philosophy called Theosophy refers to the Akashic Records as Akashic notes or Akasha's Library. It views the records as a collection of all knowledge in history stored in the etheric plane.

This collection is the holographic record of the mental space-time continuum. Regardless of the form in which it is expressed, the ancient Greeks called it the Vision of Pawn, the Chinese the Great Tao, and the Hindus the Adman Consciousness. The figures of god, goddess, and demon which appear in the early stages of awakening are recognized by Carl Jung as archetypes of the collective unconscious and are considered to be victorious from the dream by primitive people. In phenomenology, they are seen as the initial impulse, the beginning of manifestation.

Akasha's Chronicles is not only an account of everything that has happened, but which can be read by a person in doubt with special sensitivity. No, they have a tremendous influence on the development of modernity. Akasha is one of the cosmic principles; it is plastic matter creative in its physical nature, and unchanging in its physical principles. It is the quintessence of all possible forms of energy, material, psychic, and spiritual. It contains the seeds of universal creation, yielding shoots under the impulse of the Divine spirit.

The term Akasha first appears in the writings of Helena Blavatsky, which was introduced into the language of theosophy in the 19th century. She characterized it as a type of Life Force also referring to the indestructible tablets of Astral Light Recording both the past and future of human thought and action the idea of Akasha was then further explored by Alfred Percy Synod in his book : esoteric Buddhism the Buddha, teaches that those things are Eternal Akasha and Nirvana everything has come out of Akasha in obedience to its inherent law of motion and passing away nothing comes from nothing the Mahab Harada and the Purana tell of a mysterious famous verdict Sage known as

Narada The Story Goes that Narada transformed his mind in such a way that he drew information and knowledge from the source so that you could teach all of those around him great wisdom Narada had a connection to the pure knowledge that is the foundation of the cosmic order he had the ability to directly enter and receive information translated into understandable language another ancient entity that has also been in contact with the records is the Egyptian God more commonly known as thought or Hermistry's - which we will be talking in the next chapter - majestis before being designated as a god thought was the first great Egyptian philosopher discoverer of the mysterious ancient schools and altar of over 40 writings including the book of thought the Emerald Scrolls and the Divine Py Mander to the Egyptians his knowledge was so great and he was so admired by all that at first they identified him as the messenger of the Gods after a while they included him in the Egyptian Pantheon of Gods again as Tesla says the day science begins to study phenomena of a non-physical nature also it will make more progress in a decade than it has in all the previous centuries of its existence but are we even ready to reflect on these words or are we still afraid of the unknown after years spent studying the nature of electromagnetic and gravitational fields Nobel Prize nominee **Dr Erwin Laszlo** announced that he had found proof of the akashic field he starts from the discovery of the quantum zero point which is a field that exists all around us we cannot see it but we can detect it indirectly this is also shared in Albert Einstein's work we know it exists Dr Laszlo proposed that this field not only carries physical information about the physics of the universe but also a lot of information about the mental side of things according to theoretical physics the zero point is a Quantum field of waves that are invisible but exist throughout the universe space itself is made of energy and information and the way information is carried through space is by waves these waves are called Quantum waves and if the akashic field is made of these Quantum waves that are known to all forms of intelligent life which includes the human brain, the brains of extra-terrestrial, entities and all sorts of other beings that means that anyone could tap into these Quantum waves and receive information almost two decades after Laszlo's occultation Nobel prize-winning physicist Richard Feynman published his incredible work in the direction of quantum physics the strange theory of light and matter in it he develops the idea that electrons in our brains can be activated and informed by Quantum waves influencing our thoughts and our subconscious Richard also talks about the idea that subatomic particles no matter the distance between them can still influence each other through the Instant Transmission of information. Feynman also discovered that even an electron passing through our brains receives signals from the past but to compensate it should also receive signals from the future this means that every single electron in our brain is a receiver of information and once again Tesla seems to have been right when he said:" my brain is just a receiver " there is a core in the universe from which we derive knowledge powers and Inspirations I have not penetrated the secrets of this core but I know it exists

In the early 20th century scientists discovered that the laws of classical physics were not valid for small particles a new physics was born quantum physics which radically overturned previously dominant ideas any energy can only be absorbed or released in the form of small portions of quanta having a certain energy that's what Max Planck said in the 20th century a little later Albert Einstein concluded that light was a stream of quanta later called photons.

Such an experiment was carried out in 1999 by the Austrian Quantum physicist Anton Tilinger in 1999, he and his colleagues conducted an experiment in which they were able to observe the wave behavior of carbon 60 through diffraction the C60 molecule is the largest and most complex object in which wave behavior is observed the scientists shot the molecules towards a diffraction grating and on the other side they observed an interference pattern of dark and light bands on a screen this pattern only occurs when a wave passes through the grading which means that behind the wall the molecule has wave behavior, however shortly after it becomes a molecule again the interesting part was that the openings in the grading were five times larger than the molecule itself it's like going through a door that's five times wider than us and floating in space behind it and shortly after that collecting ourselves and becoming whole again. This styling gear experiment dematerializes matter and proves that everything is a wave and energy held in a certain field which apparently is also energy.

Thomas Young's experiments in 1972 and styling year 1999 confirmed that all that exists is energy all matter is energy held in a field that is energy held in energy this leads to the conclusion that it is all about frequency vibrations and the interactions between them and in 2010 Masaki Sano and his team managed to transform energy into information and prove that energy is information and information is energy they even managed to find the coefficient of this transformation stories of people experiencing strange conditions are not unknown to us in modern times, in 1923 just 12 years old while returning home little Vangelia was struck by a sudden storm she was found unconscious covered in stones and Earth she survived but lost her sight forever eventually she says that she started seeing things differently in a dream Babavanga predicted the death of King Boris III the fall of the Twin Towers the collapse of Czechoslovakia and the Soviet Union and hundreds of other individual cases of people from all over the world who visited her, she said she could see everything with the eye of her mind and that when she looked at a person, she could see their whole life in its entirety from birth to death as if she was watching a movie.

Her predictions are extremely accurate which tells us that the ability to take in information from beyond, Earth has nothing to do with the five senses we know one of those people who was apparently able to connect with the akashic field was Michelle then Nostradam better known as Nostradamus he predicted numerous events including the Great Fire of London in 1666, the French Revolution and even the rise of Adolf Hitler he claimed to have succeeded thanks to the methods used by ancient Greek oracles and Christian mysticism Nostradamus attempted to explain and speak of a Divine State in which everything happens at once and is not linear as we perceive it just as Tesla and Einstein claimed to have gotten their ideas for their great discoveries from some outside Source.

Einstein said that his theory of relativity came to him in a split second as he seem to come out of nowhere it's intriguing to know that some of the greatest discoveries in history were received as ideas at the same time by different people located in various parts of the world who had no apparent connection with each other, this suggests that the akashic records may be guiding the consciousness of humanity, there are many people who have done amazing things thanks to the Akashi Chronicles including Suji Jin from China, who can tell the story of any person just by knowing their first name according to what we can find in most spiritual books the akashic records also bear the name The Book of Life as it contains every thought word intention emotion and desire of the Soul, it is very important to understand the concept that the akashic records are actually no different that the Energy

Information potential of the universe or the unity Consciousness God the source the universal OM the collective Consciousness the universal mind. In fact we can say if it's easier to you that these are living changing documents for each of us but they do change with us they evolve with us along with the choices we make every moment to complete the picture of our own lives they contain an infinite amount of information that can always be used accessed and realized by ourselves let's imagine a forest with an infinite number of trees filled with an infinite number of delicious apples, each apple holds the key to a different experience each tree symbolizes the themes and tasks we set ourselves to be able to experience as a higher being when we want to know a particular piece of information, we simply need to connect with that particular tree and that particular Apple, they are all available to us and it is a matter of Desire for exploration development and compassion to obtain what we desire sometimes the information will not be complete and sometimes it will sound illogical but that is because it is beyond time and space therefore beyond our own understandings, limitations and filtrations of the world for example when something happens to us that we would describe as a bad situation or a difficult challenge it is usually our higher mind that gives us the opportunity to evolve, eventually we realize that we are both the higher mind the person and the source of all that is in the Oneness and it is only the focus on what we desire that also determines what will happen seen from this perspective we become The Magicians of reality that is why it is said that the akashic records are like a huge Labyrinth and it is impossible to determine their nature or their type the only objective way to read this information is to exclude the logic of what we know as the ego and how does one access the akashic records by listening inward because the answer to every question the answer how to understand his way is always within us the inner self is part of the infinite while the stubbornness of the personality which can lead us astray is always at war with the infinite because it lacks what can be called endurance fate patience then as soon as the body through which the information is transmitted is attuned to it by suppressing the Consciousness in material sheet it becomes a conduit through which the Chronicles can be read.

4

Chapter Four

"THE HOLY FREQUENCIES" | SACRED KNOWLEDGE Of Ancient Solfeggio Scale

"Sounds are the echo of the "Harmony of the Spheres" which man took into himself when he came down from the divine-spiritual world into the physical world."— Rudolf Steiner-

The Solfeggio frequencies are believed to be the holy tones that can positively impact our physical, mental, and spiritual health. These frequencies range from 174 Hertz to 963 Hertz and have a distinct vibrational signature that can be used to promote well-being. The concept of Solfeggio frequencies is based on the idea that certain sounds can influence our overall health. It is believed that these frequencies can help to create balance within our bodies and minds, and can even be used to help us heal. Many people use the Solfeggio frequencies in their everyday lives to help them stay healthy and balanced. Whether used for relaxation, meditation, or healing, the Solfeggio frequencies can be a powerful tool for promoting well-being.

The ancient solfeggio scale known as just intonation has been used in Gregorian chants for centuries, but its roots go back much further. It is believed to have originated in Biblical times and consists of a six-tone scale, with three additional tones discovered since then. Musicologists and researchers have studied the effects of this scale, and many agree that it has a positive impact on the mind and body. It is said to promote harmony and balance and can even be used to reduce stress and anxiety. The tones of just intonation are believed to be capable of inducing relaxation and peace, and can even help to reduce pain. By listening to the tones of just intonation, one can experience a sense of well-being and relaxation, as well as a heightened sense of awareness and connection to the universe. Although the effects of just intonation are still being researched, there is no doubt that it has been used to great effect in the past and co

Back in the 11th century, a Benedictine monk named Guido Diaretzo introduced the musical scale we now know as the Solfeggio frequencies. Modern research contests that the scale dates back much further, and that the monks used the original six Solfeggio notes in their Gregorian chants, which we now know consists of the frequencies 396, 417, 528, 639, 741, and 852 Hertz. Unfortunately, by the 16th century, the Solfeggio frequencies had become lost in time, and their original purpose was forgotten. However, more recently, the original frequencies have been rediscovered, and they are now known to have a profound effect on the human body and mind. It is believed that the Solfeggio frequencies can help to balance energy, reduce stress and anxiety, and promote physical and emotional well-being.

The solfeggio scale, which is thought to have disappeared during Western Europe's Middle Ages political and religious turmoil, is an important part of musical history. Many argue that more than a simple musical scale was lost when the solfeggio scale vanished. There are even some who posit conspiratorial theories, from Biblical secrets to plots by the Roman Catholic church, as to why the scale was lost. But why is this important and why should you care?

The solfeggio scale was revered by musicians for its ability to create beautiful, meaningful music. It provided a different way of tuning instruments, allowing for a more harmonious sound. Even today, many musicians use the solfeggio scale to create their music, as the tuning system still works to create a unique and powerful sound.

So, why should you care about how musicians tune their work? The solfeggio scale is an important part of musical history and understanding it can help you appreciate the musical works of the past, as well as the works of modern musicians who choose to use the scale. Additionally, understanding the solfeggio scale may even inspire you to create your own music.

The Solfeggio Scale is a set of nine electromagnetic tones believed to have the power to heal and raise human consciousness. This ancient scale is mathematically consistent with the patterns of our universe, and it has far-reaching potential. From repairing emotional trauma and opening up spiritual consciousness to deepening our relationships and altering our DNA, the Solfeggio Scale has immense potential. It works by using the atoms in our body to vibrate at specific frequencies which correspond to the Solfeggio tones. These tones are believed to restore the body and soul to its original, perfect state.

Research has shown that the Solfeggio Scale can help to reduce stress, increase emotional well-being, and promote healing. Working with the Solfeggio Scale can also help to open up spiritual awareness and develop a more profound connection with our spiritual self. It is believed that the Solfeggio Scale can even alter our DNA, allowing us to unlock our full potential and spiritual awareness. The Solfeggio Scale is an incredible tool that has the power to heal and raise our Consciousness; thus, making it a powerful tool for transformation.

Our universe is in a constant state of motion, with molecules and atoms vibrating inanimate objects, thoughts, and sounds. Even the planet we inhabit vibrates and resonates at its own frequency. Science has revealed that the number of vibrations per second is known as frequency, measured in hertz. The human ear is only capable of hearing sounds that vibrate between 20 and 20,000 hertz. The range of frequencies that we are able to hear is only a small portion of the vast number of vibrations that are happening all around us. Our universe is a place of intense vibrations, and we only get to experience a fraction of it.

The belief that certain sounds, ranging from 174 Hertz to 963 Hertz, can positively impact our mental, physical, and spiritual health forms the basis of ancient Sacred Music Traditions dating back to the 8th Century, such as the Gregorian Chants and Indian Sanskrit Chants. The Solfeggio Frequencies, commonly associated with the Gregorian Chants, are a form of monophonic sound. These frequencies, which are derived from numerical values used in ancient hymns and chants, are said to have a healing effect on the body, mind, and spirit. It is believed that listening to the frequencies of the Solfeggio can help one to achieve balance and harmony and that each frequency has a specific purpose and benefit. Through the use of these frequencies, it is believed that one can restore balance and harmony to the body, mind, and spirit.

In the 1970s, Dr. Joseph Puleo rediscovered Solfeggio frequencies, bringing their many benefits back into public awareness. His research utilized mathematical numeral reduction to identify six measurable tones that can bring the human body back into balance and aid in healing. Dr. Joseph Puleo was inspired to use Pythagorean math to examine the Book of Numbers in the Old Testament Bible. His examination of the Book of Numbers revealed a repeating pattern of the six Solfeggio tones, providing evidence of their healing power. Further research indicates that these tones may be able to restore the body to its natural state, helping to promote health and wellness. The ancient Solfeggio frequencies offer a unique opportunity to improve physical and emotional well-being, and Dr. Joseph Puleo's work has brought them back into the public eye.

Pythagoras was an ancient Greek mathematician who is well known for his Pythagorean theorem. The theorem explains the relation between the sides of a right triangle, using the equation a2 + b2 = c2. Not only was Pythagoras an important figure in mathematics, but he also had a tremendous influence on ancient Greek philosophers like Plato and Socrates. The Pythagorean method, which was used by Dr. Pulio, requires one to contemplate the relationship between numbers and the universe. Many of the philosophical discussions that took place in ancient Greece were based upon the teachings of Pythagoras. Pythagoras was the founder of the Pythagorean school of thought, which focused heavily on the philosophical implications of mathematics. The Pythagorean theorem was the cornerstone of the Pythagorean school of thought, and it has been used for centuries to explain the relationship between numbers, geometry, and the universe. Pythagoras was also responsible for introducing the concept of irrational numbers, which are numbers that cannot be expressed as a ratio of two integers. This discovery had far-reaching implications for the field of mathematics, and it is still used today. Pythagoras' contributions to mathematics and philosophy continue to inspire and influence people throughout the world.

When Dr Pulio applied this method to chapter 7 starting with verse 12, he noticed a pattern developing. Every sixth verse - 12, 18, 24, 30 - repeated the same sequence of 396 verses, 13, 19, 25, 31, and so on. This was repeated 417 times. These two frequencies, 396 and 417, formed the basis of the first two frequencies in the solfeggio. By repeating this process, Dr. Pulio uncovered a further three frequencies, now forming an extension to the scale.

The pioneering research of Dr. Pulio has uncovered three new frequencies in the scale, all of which have associated benefits. 174 Hertz is associated with pain reduction and anesthetic properties, 285 Hertz is associated with cellular repair, body regeneration, and improved immunity, and finally, 963 Hertz is associated with spiritual Awakening and connection to the Oneness of the universe. If we continue to apply the Pythagorean method to the solfeggio frequencies, we may be able to uncover further frequencies with associated benefits.

The Pythagorean method to the solfeggio frequencies is a system that reveals the underlying mathematics of the universe. It reveals that each frequency adds up to 3, 6, or 9, and two frequencies in the original scale include the numbers 3, 6, and 9. These solfeggio frequencies were believed to profoundly affect the conscious and subconscious mind in order to stimulate healing and promote vitality. Thanks to Pulio's work, and the renewed interest of many scientists, the system has been further studied and its potential utilized. It has been found to be an effective tool for improving physical, mental, and emotional well-being. By utilizing the solfeggio frequencies, one can create a positive environment for healing and spiritual growth. It is believed that through the use of the solfeggio frequencies, one can tap into higher states of consciousness and access the power of the divine. Through the use of the solfeggio frequencies, one can find peace, spiritual growth, and increased vitality.

Research conducted by musicologist Professor Willie Appel indicates that the scale was likely first introduced by Guido Direzo, a Benedictine monk. Monks of this order of the Catholic Church followed the Rule of Saint Benedict, and the earliest example of the scale was Direzo's musical rendition of the hymn to Saint John the Baptist, or UTCIS, which is based on an 8th Century poem attributed to another Monk named Paulus Diaconus. This hymn was the first example of the scale in existence, and it is believed to have been composed by Direzo himself. The scale has since become widely used in various forms of music, from classical to jazz. The original scale of UTCIS is still widely used today and continues to be a source of inspiration for many composers.

The third frequency, 528 Hertz, is said to be beneficial in restoring the balance of whole-body systems. It is believed to bring about the transformation of energy and consciousness, helping to re-align our bodies with our higher purpose. This frequency can be used to repair DNA damage and to stimulate our creativity, intuition, and intelligence. It has also been said to bring us closer to our spiritual nature, allowing us to connect with the divine and tap into our true essence.

This frequency can be used to bring us peace, harmony, and balance, allowing us to experience a greater sense of connection and well-being. It is believed to help us to heal on all levels, physical, mental, and spiritual, and can be used to help us find greater clarity and focus in our lives. By using this frequency, we can create a space of openness and trust, allowing us to move freely and be open to new possibilities.

The three frequencies, 396 Hertz, 417 Hertz, and 528 Hertz, can be used to help us move through our lives with greater ease and understanding. They can help us to heal from past traumas and liberate us from fear and guilt, and can open us up to new possibilities and experiences. By using these frequencies, we can gain a greater sense of connection and peace, and be more in touch with our true nature.

639 Hertz the fourth is believed to be a powerful frequency that can help us to improve our relationships and connections with the people around us. It is said to have the power to heal strained relationships and help us create new ones. This frequency is believed to be capable of

harmonizing our energy fields and emotional states, helping us to better relate to those around us and create a more positive atmosphere. It is believed to be a powerful tool for emotional healing, enabling us to find common ground, understanding, and mutual respect. 639 Hertz the Fourth can help us to forge new relationships and foster deeper connections with those we already know, new and old alike.

741 Hertz, the fifth of the original notes, is known as the frequency of expression and solutions. It helps us to open up and share our gifts with the world more fully. 852 Hertz, the sixth and final note, returns us to the spiritual order, improving our access to the spiritual or Sublime. Additionally, Mother Earth's natural heartbeat rhythm is the frequency of 7.83 Hertz, also known as the Schumann resonance. This frequency helps us to connect with the Earth's energy and be in harmony with the environment.

The 741 Hertz frequency is a powerful tool that allows us to open up and share our gifts with the world. Similarly, 852 Hertz brings us back to the spiritual order, helping us to reconnect with our spiritual side. And the 7.83 Hertz frequency, also known as the Schumann resonance, helps us to connect with the Earth's energy, ultimately promoting harmony with the environment. Thus, these three frequencies have the power to help us access the spiritual, connect with the environment, and share our gifts with the world.

- 741 Hertz the fifth is connected to expression and solutions helping us open up and share our gifts with the world more fully
- 852 Hertz the sixth and final of the original notes returns us to the

spiritual order improving our access to the spiritual or Sublime Mother Earth's natural heartbeat rhythm is the frequency of 7.83 Hertz also known as the Schumann resonance a 7.83 hertz.

Frequency is an alpha Theta brainwave frequency in the human brain, which is a relaxed dreamy, sleepy state. This is when cell regeneration and healing happen, making it no surprise that people nowadays, especially in bigger cities, are unbalanced, irritated, reactive and angry, and diseases are rising in astronomical numbers. This could be attributed to the electromagnetic fields generated by power supply systems, which can have an adverse effect on the brain, disrupting the natural alpha Theta brainwave frequency. To combat this, people can use various methods such as meditation, yoga, and sound bathing, to help bring the brain back into balance and restore the natural alpha Theta brainwave frequency. With the right techniques and practice, people can restore their balance and well-being and lead healthier and more fulfilling lives.

Theta brainwave frequency is a relaxed dreamy state that is essential for the body's natural healing and regeneration processes. Unfortunately, in today's world, especially in larger cities, people are becoming increasingly unbalanced and irritable, resulting in higher levels of anger and disease. This is largely due to the electromagnetic fields generated by power supply systems, telecommunications appliances, computers and other forms of technology. These fields affect our brain waves and disrupt our natural balance, leading to physical and mental health issues. It is therefore important that we take steps to limit our exposure to these electromagnetic fields, in order to help maintain our overall health and well-being.

The Solfeggio frequencies have been used to bring about positive effects in people for many years. They resonate in harmony with the Schumann Resonance of eight Hertz, which is the natural frequency of the Earth. Musically speaking, the frequencies are derived by beginning at 8 Hertz and working up the musical scale octave until the C note is vibrating at the 256-hertz frequency and the A note is vibrating at 432 Hertz. When music is tuned to harmonize with this frequency, it is known as the “Solfeggio frequency.” This type of tuning is believed to bring about a sense of peace and relaxation. Additionally, research suggests that these frequencies may restore balance to the body, reduce stress levels, and increase self-awareness. In addition, the frequencies are believed to create an environment of healing and increased well-being. For these reasons, many people turn to Solfeggio frequencies to achieve a sense of balance and harmony.

Scientific experiments have proven that tuning into 7.83 Hertz, the planet's own magnetic frequency, can provide a host of benefits to people, such as enhanced learning, improved memory, body rejuvenation, improved balance, increased stress tolerance, anti-jet lag, anti-mind control, and grounding. Conversely, experiments were done where Schumann resonances, or exposure to the 7.83 Hertz frequency, was removed from an individual's environment. The results of these experiments showed that exposure to this frequency is integral to the well-being of individuals. Therefore, it is essential to maintain access to this frequency in order to benefit from its effects.

The results of a recent study were astounding. When the 7.83-hertz frequency was removed from the individual's environment, the subjects reported experiencing migraine headaches, emotional distress, and other health problems. This shows just how important it is to be in tune with the Earth's magnetic frequency.

The Earth's magnetic frequency is a subtle energy that resonates within the environment. It is believed to be a vital part of the energy that makes up life on Earth. When this frequency is disrupted, it can have a negative effect on the health and well-being of individuals.

The study conducted on the effect of 7.83-hertz frequency is a testament to the power of this energy. The results demonstrate the importance of maintaining a harmonious relationship with the Earth's natural energy.

The results of this study illustrate the importance of being aware of the environment we inhabit. We must be mindful of the subtle energies that flow through our lives and make sure to stay in tune with the Earth's magnetic frequency. By doing so, we can protect our health and well-being from any potential disturbances.

Sound healing is a powerful practice that helps to bring our bodies and minds back into alignment with the Earth's magnetic frequency. By using sound, we are able to restore ourselves to a natural state where our bodies can take care of themselves and our own natural immune systems can do their job. Sound healing has been used for thousands of years, and it is still often used today to help with physical and mental ailments. It is important to be in tune with the Earth's magnetic frequency and to use sound healing as part of our self-care routine. It can help us to feel more relaxed and energized, as well as better able to cope with life's challenges. Sound healing can also help us to reconnect with ourselves and find a sense of inner peace. Taking the time to listen to the sound of the Earth can help us to find balance and harmony in our lives.

In the 1970s, researchers discovered that exposure to solfeggio tones had an interesting effect on the DNA in cells - they were able to better absorb ultraviolet light without any resulting damage. This revelation helps us to understand the natural process of strengthening our bodies and becoming in tune with our environment. The use of a Delta frequency tuning fork provides the opportunity to observe the effects of solfeggio tones on DNA more closely. It is clear that this is a field of research that is continuing to yield fascinating results, and as time goes on, we will gain more insight into how solfeggio tones can be used to strengthen the body.

A recent study by researchers found that people exposed to sound at 432 Hertz experienced lower blood pressure and breathing rates. It was also reported that they felt more satisfied when listening to this frequency. Sound healing has been used as a natural anaesthetic to help relieve pain, as one study found that sounds of 432 Hertz were beneficial in reducing dental anxiety and relieving pain during dental surgery. This indicates that sound healing has the potential to be used as an effective form of pain management. Further research is needed to explore the use of sound healing as an alternative to traditional forms of pain relief.

The feeling of relief during dental surgery is palpable. As we become absorbed in the moment, a kind of peaceful rejuvenation takes over. Wind rustling in the trees produces a cacophony of sound with woodwinds, strings, horns, and timpani all joining in the ruckus. This symphony of nature allows us to forget the pain and anxiety of our dental procedure, allowing us to relax and enjoy the moment. In this way, the natural world provides us with an escape and a source of comfort during dental surgery.

When musicians tune their instruments with precision, the sound that resonates is like a wave that brings peace and excitement unlike any other. Skydiving and exploring secret caves may provide a thrilling experience, but nothing can compare to the serenity of a perfectly in-tune ensemble. The human body functions similarly; if one part is out of sync, it can lead to an array of ailments. When everything is in harmony, however, there is a sense of balance and well-being that can be found nowhere else.

Dr. John Baliu ND Ph.D., an expert in the field of electromagnetic color spectrum and sound systems, explains that according to Dr. Leonard Horowitz, there is only one number in the entire numbering system where both of these systems are in harmony. That number is 528. Dr. Horowitz has found that this number holds an essential connection between the two systems. He believes that it is this number that holds the key to unlocking the secrets of the universe, and unlocking the potential for greater health and well-being. 528 is a number of immense power and potential, and it is the goal of Dr. Horowitz to help unlock its secrets.

In 2018, Akimoto and Yamaguchi conducted a study to examine the effect of 528 Hertz music on the endocrine system and the autonomic nervous system. Objective and subjective measures were used to assess the effect, including salivary biomarkers, an electrocardiogram, and a mood state questionnaire. Nine healthy participants, one male and eight females, aged 26 to 37 years, took part in the experiment. The participants listened to 528 Hertz and standard 440 Hertz music on separate days. The results of the study showed that 528 Hertz music had a positive effect on the endocrine system and the autonomic nervous system. It was concluded that 528 Hertz music has a positive effect on the endocrine and autonomic nervous system, and further research is needed to confirm the findings.

Before and after exposure to music, the activity of the autonomic nervous system was continuously recorded and the Profile of Mood States Second Edition (POMS-II) was administered as a subjective indicator of stress in the 528 Hertz condition. Results showed that mean cortisol levels significantly decreased, chromogranin A tended to decrease and oxytocin significantly increased after music exposure.

However, no significant change was observed in the other measures. These results suggest that music exposure has the potential to reduce stress and anxiety, as indicated by the changes in the autonomic nervous system activity, cortisol levels, and oxytocin levels. Future research is needed to further understand the effect of music on the autonomic nervous system and its potential to reduce stress.

The results of a recent study indicate that exposure to both types of music had a significant effect on the ratio of low-frequency to high-frequency autonomic nervous system activity. Specifically, this ratio decreased significantly after exposure to both types of music. In addition, the coefficient of variation of RR intervals also decreased significantly, but only after exposure to 528 Hertz music. Finally, tension, anxiety, and total mood disturbance scores were significantly reduced after exposure to 528 Hertz music. These results suggest that exposure to 528 Hertz music in particular may be beneficial in reducing stress and tension levels.

Research has found that there was no significant difference in the autonomic nervous system and endocrine system following 440 Hertz music. These results suggest that the influence of music on these systems varies depending on the frequency of the music. Furthermore, it has been found that 528 Hertz music has an especially strong stress-reducing effect, even after just five minutes of exposure. Researchers found that stress levels were reduced following the five minutes of exposure. This shows that music can have a powerful effect on reducing stress levels, even with such a short duration.

This study has revealed a significant difference in the impact of music on the nervous system. Specifically, whereas the traditional 440 Hz music has not had any significant effect, the 528 Hz music has been observed to lead to a decrease in mean levels of cortisol and an increase in mean levels of oxytocin. This finding indicates that music and sound can be used to heal Post-Traumatic Stress Disorder (PTSD) by its impact on the nervous system. The use of Solfeggio frequencies has been seen to be particularly useful in this regard. This study, therefore, proves that music and sound can be used as therapeutic tool to help heal PTSD.

285 Hertz is associated with cellular repair, which helps the body's tissue and organs to regenerate. This cellular repair is also beneficial to the skin, assisting in the healing of burns, lacerations, and other types of damage. Additionally, cellular repair is natally linked to the immune system, where the health of B and T cells is vitally important for fighting off viruses and diseases. The 285 Hertz tone has been shown to improve our health and overall well-being. It helps to stimulate the repair of damaged cells, which in turn leads to faster healing of wounds and improved functioning of the immune system. The tone is also thought to reduce inflammation and improve the body's ability to absorb vitamins and minerals. Therefore, by listening to the 285 Hertz tone, we can improve our physical and mental health.

At 174 Hertz, the lowest tone has a great influence on us, not only on a mental and emotional level but also on the physical plane. This tone has been noted to act as a natural anaesthetic, helping to reduce pain both physically and energetically. It has also been observed to give our organs a greater sense of security. This low tone helps us to relax and feel safe in our physical bodies, allowing us to better take care of our overall health.

174 Hertz has a powerful effect on our physical and energetic bodies. It works as a natural anaesthetic, helping to relieve pain and discomfort, while also creating a feeling of safety and security. The highest frequency of the Solfeggio scale is 963 Hertz, and this frequency is believed to connect us with the perfection and unity of the Universe. It is said that this frequency holds the power to transform our consciousness and open us up to spiritual growth. By opening ourselves to this frequency, we can unlock deep inner wisdom and a greater understanding of the Universe.

The last of the Solfeggio frequencies is 963 Hertz, which takes us to the highest plane of consciousness. This frequency connects us to the perfection of the universe, allowing us to tap into the Oneness that permeates everything that is and will be. This frequency relates to the crown chakra, which is linked to the pineal gland, the central nervous system through which we can access higher intuition. This frequency allows us to open up to the power of the universe, allowing us to move past our physical limitations and be more connected to the spiritual realm. Through this connection, we can better understand our purpose in life and have a deeper connection with the divine. We can also gain insight into our spiritual path and the paths of others. The 963 Hertz frequency can be used for meditation and prayer to help us open up to the power of the universe and to access higher levels of consciousness. With this frequency, we can create a deeper connection to the divine and become more aware of our inner spirit.

The original six Solfeggio frequencies are 396 Hertz, 417 Hertz, 528 Hertz, 639 Hertz, 741 Hertz, and 852 Hertz. Each frequency is believed to have its own unique benefits. 396 Hertz is associated with liberating guilt and fear. 417 Hertz is associated with undoing situations and facilitating change. 528 Hertz is associated with transformation and miracles, including the ability to repair DNA. 639 Hertz is associated with connecting and balancing relationships. 741 Hertz is associated with solving problems and expressions of creativity. 852 Hertz is associated with returning to spiritual order. All of these frequencies are believed to be able to help us to unlock our full potential.

Frequencies in music that are believed to have a more powerful effect on the body and mind. These are known as Solfeggio Frequencies and have been around for centuries, appearing in ancient texts, music, and spiritual rituals. The Solfeggio Frequencies are believed to have healing power, and when combined with music, they can be used to create a powerful resonance in the body. This resonance is thought to have a positive effect on the body, mind, and spirit. Furthermore, music with

Solfeggio Frequencies is believed to bring balance and harmony to a person's emotional and physical states. This is why many people choose to listen to music with Solfeggio Frequencies to relax and restore balance. Additionally, the Solfeggio Frequencies can be used to create a positive environment that promotes peace and well-being. Ultimately, musical frequency is not just a form of vibration, it is also a powerful tool for healing, relaxation, and spiritual growth.

The Benedictine monks of the 11th century found solace in tuning their chants to the solfeggio scale. These chants were their prayers to a higher power, and they chose tones that resonated with their spiritual energy. The Solfeggio scale is renowned for its ability to influence and transform well-being. It can help to reduce emotional and physical ills, as well as create a deeper spiritual connection with the universe. Sound healing is the practice of using tones, frequencies, and vibrations to clear blockages and create a sense of balance and harmony. It is believed that this method of healing has been used since ancient times, and is still practiced today. Through sound healing, one can tap into the spiritual source of healing, allowing for a deeper connection to the universe.

Solfeggio music is undeniably beneficial in helping to manage a number of conditions including anxiety, depression, post-traumatic stress disorder, autism, and dementia. Its calming and relaxing effects make it highly useful for use during meditation. It can be difficult to achieve a peaceful and meditative mind state without external guidance, but using the frequencies of solfeggio music can make it easier. Listening to solfeggio can help to bring the body and mind into a state of balance and relaxation, helping to reduce the symptoms of the aforementioned conditions. Whether it's used during a focused meditation session or just in the background of everyday life, solfeggio music can be an effective aid in achieving a peaceful mental state.

If you are looking for a way to help you relax and meditate, then binaural beats combined with sound bath meditation may be the perfect solution. Binaural beats are two different tones played in each ear that trick the brain into hearing a third, blended tone. This blended tone encourages the brain to enter a meditative state, making it easier for you to reach the desired effect. Additionally, you can also listen to Solfeggio frequencies during your sound bath meditation. These frequencies are said to have healing properties, and when combined with binaural beats, can be a powerful tool for relaxation and meditation.

5

Chapter Five

The Secret POWER Of DNA

PART 1

"For what lies inside the human being is the whole spiritual cosmos in condensed form. In our inner organism we have an image of the entire cosmos".
Rudolf Steiner

An exploration of DNA's power is presented in this chapter.

Activating something that sounds like a mystical statement can seem like a miraculous event, but in actuality, it's quite simple. Although some may already know how to do it, for others, it may be an astonishing experience. It could be something as small as turning a switch or pressing a button, yet the outcome can be just as grand. It's amazing what a few small steps can do.

produced by the cells, and the process is carried out by a series of transcription and translation steps.

The DNA strands are arranged in structures called chromosomes, and the chromosomes contain the genetic information that is passed down from one generation to the next. This information is known as the gene, and it is responsible for the characteristics that are inherited. For example, if a person has a gene for eye color, then they will have blue eyes.

In addition to the genes, the DNA strands also contain other pieces of information such as regulatory elements that control the expression of the genes. This is what makes each individual unique, as the regulatory elements can be very different between individuals.

Overall, DNA is the fundamental building block of life, and it is responsible for the hereditary traits passed down from one generation to the next. It is made up of nucleotides, which contain the genetic information that is passed down. It is arranged in structures called chromosomes, and the chromosomes contain the genetic information that is passed down from one generation to the next. It also contains other pieces of information such as regulatory elements that control the expression of the genes. Understanding how DNA works is essential in order to understand how to reprogram ourselves and unlock our full potential.

Real zeros and ones are the fundamental building blocks of modern technology. They are what make our phones and computers work. Bits of data, also known as binary code, are made up of zeros and ones and can be used to store information. This is why scientists are now looking into the possibility of using DNA to store zeros and ones. DNA is a powerful storage medium that could allow scientists to store and process data in a more efficient way. By using DNA to store zeros and ones, scientists would be able to store more data than ever before. This would revolutionize the way we store and process data, allowing us to create even more powerful technology than we have today.

George Church and Chris Shuri have conducted a remarkable experiment that has the potential to revolutionize our understanding of data storage. By downloading one of their books and one of their e-books onto the DNA and then uploading it from the DNA back to the server again, they have successfully transferred digital bits of information directly onto DNA and uploaded it back again. This means that we are now literally walking around with our own miniature data storage devices. The implications of this discovery could be far-reaching, as it could help to solve many of the current challenges in data storage. It could potentially bring data storage into the realm of the small and the affordable, making it much easier to store and access data.

Furthermore, this experiment could potentially have a huge impact on the medical field, allowing for the long-term storage of genetic information. All in all, George Church and Chris Shuri have made an incredible discovery that could have a major impact on the future of data storage.

The sheer amount of data that can be stored in a single gram of DNA is astonishing. It is estimated that a single gram can contain up to 433 petabytes of data – 700 Tetabytes, which is equivalent to over 70 billion copies of an e-book. It is astonishing to think that such a small amount of matter can contain this much data – enough to store the entire universe within. It is truly remarkable to think that we can store so much information within such a small space.

It's truly amazing to think that our bodies can store so much information. Every single molecule, atom, and particle inside of us has been around since the beginning of time, and all of this information is stored inside of us, right now. This means that we have the entire universe—13.5 billion years' worth of data—inside of us. It's a staggering thought and a reminder of the incredible power of the human body. It's also a reminder that we are indeed a part of the universe; when people say that the universe is inside of us, it's not just a figure of speech. The universe is literally inside of us.

According to the law of thermodynamics, energy cannot be disordered or destroyed, but simply transformed. This means that all of the particles and bits of data that were present from the beginning are still around right now, recycled, and reused again and again. Atoms are also recycled and reused, and even though they may take on different forms, they are all connected to the same energy source. Everything, from the beginning of time to now, is all one single connected energy source that is constantly in a state of transformation. This means that you, as an individual, are a product of this same energy source - your form is merely a temporary result of the energy's transformation. Therefore, you are here right now, at this moment, in this particular form of the energy's transformation.

This theory has been the subject of much debate and discussion, and its validity has yet to be proven. Proponents of the theory cite circumstantial evidence such as the similarities between the Sumerian and Babylonian texts and the descriptions of the Anunnaki. Critics of the theory point out the lack of scientific evidence to support the claims.

Regardless of its validity, the Anunnaki Theory is an interesting concept that has been the source of much conjecture. It is possible that the Anunnaki did, in fact, come to Earth and splice in an additional 98% of our DNA, giving us the advanced capabilities that we now possess. Whether or not this is true is still a matter of debate.

The ancient Sumerian texts have long been studied for their insight into the origins of humanity. In particular, the Epic of Gilgamesh and The Emerald Tablets provide evidence that our ancestors were already advanced enough to understand genetics and even to genetically modify other species to serve their needs. One such species was believed to be an ancestor of Homo sapiens, which may have been modified to create a slave species. This ancient knowledge is still being studied to this day, and the implications of such practices are far-reaching. It is clear that the Sumerian texts offer a unique perspective into our past, and will continue to be a source of fascination for many years to come.

The answer to why our DNA was unplugged is not an easy one, and it has perplexed scientists and historians for many years. It is believed that our DNA was unplugged by those who sought to make us into a slave race and make us do their work for them. This unplugged DNA is now referred to as 'junk DNA', but it is anything but junk. In fact, it is unplugged DNA, and the fact that it was unplugged is actually an even greater mystery. It is believed that the unplugging of our DNA was done to restrict our biological and spiritual potential, but the exact reason remains unknown. Many theories have been proposed to explain why our DNA was unplugged, but none of them have been proven. Whatever the reason, the unplugging of our DNA has had a profound impact on human history and our future

Ancient people had the capability to access their brains with magnetite crystals. This is something that we have not been taught, but the truth is these people were much more intelligent than us. It isn't just in terms of technology either; they were spiritually smarter and more in tune with nature, the universe, and the planet itself. It is known that they had bigger brains than us, which has been proven by the discovery of their skulls. They had a greater human resonant frequency than we do, which allowed them to access their brains and tap into the energies of the Earth. It is through this that we can learn more about the depths of our ancestors and the knowledge they had.

Humans have long been fascinated with the idea of our species having a spiritual antenna, and it is possible that the skulls found all over the planet suggest that those with bigger brains had bigger pineal glands. This could explain why we have billions of magnetite crystals in our brains, although we are not currently using them. It is possible that those from the past had access to these magnetite crystals, similar to how turtles use them to navigate the oceans and come back to where they need to lay their eggs. This could be the key to unlocking the secrets of our spiritual antenna and could be the answer to our ancient mystery.

Humans and animals alike have the capability to detect danger, but humans are often slow to act on it. This is evident when looking at a tsunami: wild animals have an instinctive ability to sense its approach and flee to higher ground, while humans often remain in its path and risk being swept away. This demonstrates the disconnect between our physical senses and our mental understanding of potential risks. In such cases, it can be beneficial to take cues from nature and pay attention to our instincts. If we take the time to pay attention to the warning signs, we can save ourselves from becoming a victim of a tsunami's destructive power.

For centuries, humanity has been searching for answers to the mysteries of our existence. Recently, science has uncovered a startling discovery: embedded in our very DNA is a 'worship gene'. This gene dates back to around 200,000 years ago, and its origin is unknown.

This revelation has caused us to re-examine our connection to the universe and our place in it. Our species has been severed from its source, and this disconnection has resulted in a decrease in our collective consciousness. We are no longer as aware of our connection with the universe as we once were.

This discovery has left us pondering our purpose and our true identity. What does this gene mean for us, and how can we use it to reconnect with the source of our being? As we search for answers, we must strive to rediscover our true identity and to re-establish our connection with the universe.

We may never know who embedded this gene in our DNA, but the fact remains that it is part of our very essence. It is up to us to use this knowledge to reconnect with our source and reclaim our power.

Humanity has been disconnected from its true self for a long time. We have been living in a state of reduced consciousness, unaware of our true potential. Recent scientific discoveries have uncovered a gene that is believed to be a worship gene, embedded into the human genome around 200,000 years ago. We may never know who implanted this gene into our DNA, but it is clear that we have been disconnected from our true power and potential for an incredibly long time. It is time now to reconnect with our true selves and embrace our full potential.

At the same time as this discovery, scientists have also determined the significance of telomere caps, sometimes referred to as the 'Fountain of Youth'. Telomeres are a special region of DNA found at the end of chromosomes that protect genetic information. Without telomere caps, the end of the chromosome would break off and the genetic information would be lost. Telomere caps allow chromosomes to replicate faithfully, ensuring the stability of genetic information.

The telomere caps play a vital role in cell division and aging. As cells divide, the telomere caps shorten. When the telomeres become too short, the cell can no longer divide and instead, enters a state of senescence. This lack of cell division leads to aging. It is hypothesized that telomere caps may be related to the maximum lifespan of an organism.

Telomere caps also have implications in cancer research. Telomerase, a special enzyme, can extend telomere caps. This enzyme is found in high levels in cancer cells, allowing them to replicate quickly and form tumors. Research into telomere caps and telomerase could lead to new treatments for cancer.

In summary, telomere caps are essential for the stability of genetic information and the replication of cells. Understanding the significance of telomere caps can lead to advances in medicine and science, helping to unravel the mysteries of aging and possibly even finding a cure for cancer.

It has long been speculated that the origins of the genetic modification of hominids on the planet date back hundreds of thousands of years. Recent discoveries have made it possible to pinpoint the time of the first such modification to 200,000 years ago. This discovery was made by Harvard scientists in the United States.

The scientists also discovered that, under the most ideal and pristine conditions, human beings can live for up to 120 years. This is a remarkable scientific breakthrough as it gives us greater insight into the potential life span of human beings in the future. It also allows us to understand the effects of environment and lifestyle choices on longevity.

The Bible, Sumerian texts, and other ancient sources all agree that living a healthy life should naturally lead to a lifespan of 120 years or more. So why is it that we are still dying much younger than that? It is clear that something is preventing us from reaching our full lifespan potential. This is where the discussion of GMOs, genetically modified seeds, and tortured meat comes in. These elements of modern life are believed to be contributing to our shorter lifespans by polluting our environment and causing health problems. It is obvious that more research is needed in order to determine the exact causes of our shorter lifespans and find ways to combat them.

Chromosome number two and the telomere Caps are an integral part of the cell's DNA. These telomere caps act as a buffer, allowing genetic information to stay intact when the cells and DNA replicate. This buffer material prevents any information from being lost in the transference. It is this buffer material that makes the telomere Caps so important when it comes to DNA replication. Without it, a lot of information could be lost in the process of replication.

Epigenetic Memories Run 14 Generations Deep Within DNA

Have you ever stopped to consider why you have an irrational fear of something or why you feel so strongly about a certain activity? It turns out that scientists have recently come to the realization that our epigenetic memories can be passed down through DNA for up to 14 generations. This means that the experiences, beliefs, and behaviors of our ancestors may still be present in our genetic code and influence our thoughts and feelings today. This may explain why we feel so strongly about certain activities and why some of us have an inexplicable fear of things that we have never even encountered before. This knowledge is a fascinating phenomenon that is worth considering and exploring further.

For example, if your great-great-great-great-great-grandparents experienced a traumatic event, their memories of it may still be present in your DNA. This could explain why you have a phobia of a certain place or situation, even if you have never experienced it

It is believed that the memories of our ancestors may be passed down through our DNA. This suggests that if our great-great-great-great-great-grandparents experienced a traumatic event, we could still be feeling the effects of it in some way today. This could explain a fear or phobia of certain places or situations, even if we have never experienced them ourselves.

In a similar manner, we may be drawn to activities that our ancestors were passionate about, even if we have never been exposed to them. This could be seen in the way we take an interest in certain hobbies, sports or even professions, even though we may have no prior experience or knowledge of them.

This phenomenon of inherited memories and traits is fascinating, and it provides an interesting insight into the way our experiences are passed down from generation to generation. It suggests that even though we may never have known our ancestors, their memories and personalities still live on in us.

Regardless, it is incredible to think that the memories of our ancestors could still be influencing us today. It is a reminder of the interconnectedness of life on this planet and of the power of genetics.

DNA, Quantum Entanglement & The Law Of Attraction

The Law of Attraction is an idea that states that our thoughts and beliefs can shape our reality. It suggests that we can manifest our desired outcomes by focusing on positive thoughts. This notion has been around for centuries, but it has been popularized in recent years by books, movies, and speakers.

But how does this work with the Law of Attraction? What does DNA have to do with the Law of Attraction? It turns out that the Law of Attraction is actually initiated through the DNA.

DNA is the blueprint of all life. Every cell in the body has the same blueprint, and this blueprint contains instructions for how the body should function. It is the source of all information and knowledge, and it is the basis for the Law of Attraction. When we focus our thoughts and beliefs in a certain direction, our DNA will respond by initiating the Law of Attraction.

When we focus on positive thoughts, our DNA will receive a signal to create more of what we desire. For example, if we focus on feeling happy and content, our DNA will begin to create more of that feeling. Likewise, if we focus on feeling angry and frustrated, our DNA will create more of that feeling.

The Law of Attraction is an incredibly powerful tool that can be used to manifest our desired outcomes. It works because our DNA is the source of all information and knowledge. By focusing our thoughts and beliefs in a certain direction, we can create the life of our dreams.

By raising our frequency through love, we are able to quantum entangle ourselves with the universe, allowing us to access the power and wisdom held within it. When we are in this state, we can access a higher level of understanding and insight into the deeper truths of our lives and the world around us.

When we open our hearts to love, we can access the divine energy of the universe and activate the Christ Consciousness inside us. By connecting with the divine energy of the universe, we can become one with the universe and access its limitless power and infinite wisdom.

Scientists have now uncovered an incredible discovery - our DNA is capable of sending and receiving wireless signals! This means that we have a built-in Wi-Fi system in our bodies, broadcasting information up to ten feet away from us. What's more, we are constantly downloading information from the Ether. This is an amazing breakthrough and opens the door to a wealth of potential new medical and technological applications. It could revolutionize the way we think about our own bodies, and how we interact with the world around us.

Human beings have the unique ability to tap into the Ether of space-time, an enigmatic cosmic force that is constantly transmitting information. This transmission is available to us at all times, regardless of our physical location. By being within 8 to 10 feet of the body, we can access this transmission of information and gain insight into the mysteries of the universe. This transmission is something that is always available to us, allowing us to tap into the knowledge and power of the Ether of space-time anytime we choose.

This Ether of space-time is a powerful force, one that can be used to access knowledge and information from the universe. It is a mysterious force that can be used to gain insight into the unknown and uncover hidden truths. By tapping into this force, humans can gain understanding and insight into the mysteries of the universe.

In conclusion, humans have the unique ability to tap into the Ether of space-time, a cosmic force that is constantly transmitting information. By being within 8 to 10 feet away from the human body, we can access this transmission and gain insight into the mysteries of the universe. This incredible ability to access the Ether of space-time allows humans to uncover hidden knowledge and understand the universe.

What makes the Ether of space-time so remarkable is the fact that it exists outside of our limited spectrum of perception. We can't physically see it, touch it, smell it, or hear it, yet its presence can be felt throughout the universe. It is an invisible force that is constantly at work, exerting its influence on all matter in the cosmos. Its power is believed to be responsible for the formation of galaxies, stars, and planets, and it also plays a role in the evolution of life. It is the bridge between the physical and spiritual realms, and its energy can be used to travel through time and space. The Ether of space-time is a mysterious and wondrous phenomenon, one that has captivated our imaginations for centuries.

The Ether is also believed to be responsible for the phenomenon of time dilation, which is the idea that time passes more slowly when measured near an object with a large amount of mass. This effect has been observed numerous times and is thought to be caused by Ether's influence over space-time.

The Ether of space-time is an incredibly mysterious and powerful force, and its influence and effects are still being studied and researched today. Its remarkable power and strength are undeniable, and its potential to shape our understanding of the universe and its workings is immense.

We are only able to perceive a small fraction of what lies within the Ether, and yet it contains the entire fabric of existence. In essence, we are all living within a giant hologram.

The Adinkra Codes (The Etheric Search Engine We Receive Downloads From)

The concept of space-time is one that has been studied for many years. It wasn't until recently, however, that a researcher by the name of Chika

Okoye made a breakthrough discovery. He found that space-time actually operates on something called Adinkra codes. These codes are mathematical in nature and are believed to have been used by ancient cultures such as the Dogon. They are a complex set of rules that govern the behavior of space-time and those who study them can gain a better understanding of how space-time works. Adinkra codes are an intriguing area of study, and it's exciting to think that more discoveries could be made in the near future.

Adinkra codes are used in many aspects of Dogon life, from the spiritual to the secular. They are used for divination, healing, and for various ceremonies. Adinkra codes are also used to communicate with the spirits and the ancestors. This is done by writing down the codes and then burning the paper as an offering.

The Dogon tribe in Mali Africa is believed to be the original Egyptians from the land of Khem, known today as Egypt. This is evidenced by the Dinker-codes associated with the Dogon, which are codes used to track and trace their history, which in turn can be traced back to Khem. The Dogon have kept their culture and traditions alive throughout the centuries, and their language, art, and mythology continue to tell the story of their ancient origins. Their oral histories and stories of a great flood and other events of ancient Egypt are still part of their culture today. Even their astronomical knowledge of Sirius, the companion star of our own sun, is believed to have been handed down from the original Egyptians. It is believed that the Dogon were the original inhabitants of Khem, the land of the pharaohs and that the Dinker-codes are proof of this.

James S Gates Jr is an acclaimed specialist in supersymmetry and theoretical physics. He is recognized as one of the leading figures in this field and is widely respected. In order to further his research, he has brought together an impressive team of quantum physicists to delve into the mysterious ether of space-time. Together, they are exploring the unknown, trying to uncover the secrets of what is within us and around us. What is this space-time? What is the true nature of space? This team is determined to find out.

Quantum entanglement is a real phenomenon in physics. It occurs when two particles, such as photons, are placed on the same frequency. This can be done through a process called parabolic down conversion. Once the two particles have the same frequency, they remain connected, no matter the distance between them. If one particle is taken to the other end of the universe, the change in its information would be reflected in the particle that remains local. This connection between two particles is one of the most fascinating aspects of quantum mechanics.

Correcting codes is the very foundation of the Internet, allowing search engine browsers and websites to run properly. But what about the governing force behind our space-time reality in the third dimension? It turns out that the same software programs that power websites and search engines are responsible for this. This has been peer-reviewed and accepted as science, so it's worth paying attention to. What this means is that you are capable of tapping into the vast range of information already available on the Internet, and downloading it into your body. It's an incredible power and one that you can use to create a better future for yourself.

The idea of particle energy syncing up with universal Consciousness is an idea that has been gaining traction in recent years. This is because of the concept of quantum entanglement, which allows particles to interact with each other even when separated by vast distances. This means that particles on one side of the universe can be connected with those on the other side, creating what is known as a 'quantum link'. This means that it is possible to be 'quantum entangled' directly with the 'Flower of Life', which is the face of God.

This phenomenon can be compared to the theory of relativity proposed by Albert Einstein. It states that when there is a massive object in space, such as a planet, the space around it will become warped, creating a gravitational field. Similarly, when a quantum link is created between two distant particles, the space between them will become warped, creating a powerful connection. This link allows the particles to interact in ways that would not have been possible if they were not connected.

The implications of this are far-reaching, as the particles can now communicate with each other in ways that were previously impossible. This means that the particles can now 'sync up' with the Universal Consciousness, allowing for an even deeper understanding of the universe and its workings. This opens up a world of possibilities for humanity, as we can now explore the mysteries of the universe in ways that were never before possible.

Einstein's Theory of Relativity has revolutionized our understanding of the Universe and how it works. It explains how gravity warps the space-time continuum, and how objects move in relation to each other. It also explains how Quantum Entanglement ties together particles across the universe, allowing them to interact with each other in a way that is seemingly impossible. This means that the mind is now literally warping the Ether of space itself, and the things we want in life can be created by our own consciousness. Our thoughts, emotions, and intentions can now become reality, as they are affecting the very fabric of the Universe. By understanding the power of our minds, we can use this knowledge to create the life we desire, as the things we look for are now falling toward us due to the warping of space-time. We can use this power to our advantage and create the life we have always dreamed of.

PART 2

YHVH ETERNAL ENCODED IN OUR DNA

Another Incredible discovery of our DNA:

A team of scientists found an incredible discovery when they explored the ancient spiritual text known as Sefar Yetzicah. This text had only been translated into English once but held a mysterious message that remained hidden until they uncovered it. Each alphabet has its own mysterious numerical representation and the scientists decided to use this to their advantage. They took the alphabet and replaced the elements of the DNA with their corresponding number. The result was extraordinary, as the message within the text was revealed in its entirety. This discovery has the potential to revolutionize the way we view our genetic code and the secrets that it holds. Truly, the DNA holds a message waiting to be unlocked.

The YHVH is an acronym for a Hebrew phrase meaning "Yahweh, He Causes to Be". It is used to refer to the God of the Bible, who is described as the creator and sustainer of the universe. The phrase is derived from the first two words of the Hebrew phrase, "Yahweh Hu Ha'Elohim", which translates to "The Lord is God". The YHVH acronym is often seen in religious texts, as well as religious art, and is a reminder that God is the ultimate source of power and authority. The YHVH is a reminder of the power and authority of God and a reminder of His love and care for His people.

The mysterious power of YHVH, the Eternal One, is encoded within us all. Our DNA carries the secrets of this divine power, connecting us to something far greater than ourselves. This power is an ancient source of divine wisdom, a source of healing, guidance, and understanding. The code of YHVH is a key to unlocking our true potential, both as individuals and as a collective. It is said that the code of YHVH is the key to understanding our true nature and our purpose in life. It is a reminder of the power of the divine and a reminder of the importance of reverence and respect for all life. We are all part of the same cosmic energy, and the code of YHVH is the expression of this power within us. By exploring and understanding the code of YHVH, we can learn to live in harmony with the divine and all of life.

6
Chapter Six

SIMULATED REALITY

"The Matrix is the world that has been pulled over your eyes to blind you from the truth." -Morpheus

We are living in a simulated reality, often referred to as The Matrix. The Matrix is a computer-generated world, a construct of our own minds. We all inhabit this virtual world, where the rules of physics, chemistry, and the laws of nature are all manipulated by a computer algorithm.

The Matrix is a construct of our own imaginations, a construct that allows us to explore the possibilities of what could be, what could have been, and what might be. We can create our own worlds, and explore them from within the simulated environment of The Matrix.

The Matrix is a place where we can explore our creative potential, push the boundaries of our imagination, and experience the world in a way that could not be possible in the physical world. We can create stories, universes, and characters that exist only within the framework of The Matrix. We can also access information and knowledge that is otherwise inaccessible in the physical world.

The Matrix is a place where we can expand our understanding of the universe and of ourselves. We can explore the limits of our creativity and our capabilities, and discover new ways of thinking and being. We can create our own realities and explore the possibilities of what could be, and what could have been.

The Matrix is a virtual world, where we can experience the world in a way that could not be experienced in the physical world. We can explore the boundaries of our imagination, discover the depths of our creativity, and push the limits of our understanding. We can create our own realities and explore the possibilities of what could be. We can also access knowledge and information that is otherwise inaccessible in the physical world.

The Matrix is a place where we can explore our creative potential and experience the world in a way that could not be possible in the physical world. We can create stories, universes, and characters that exist only within the framework of The Matrix. We can also access information and knowledge that is otherwise inaccessible in the physical world.

The Matrix is a virtual world, a simulated reality, and a place where we can explore the possibilities of what could be, what could have been, and what might be. We can explore the boundaries of our imagination, discover the depths of our creativity, and push the limits of our understanding. We can also access knowledge and information that is otherwise inaccessible in the physical world. We are living in a simulation called The Matrix.

We're living in a MATRIX written on mathematics called ADINKRA CODES"

"Nothing exists except through human consciousness"

George Orwell, 1984

We are living in a fascinating world, where mathematics takes on a new form. The mysterious and powerful Adinkra Codes are written in a mathematical language called Adinkra Symbols, which is used to express complex ideas, emotions, and beliefs. These symbols are believed to have originated in the Akan people of Ghana and are now used throughout the world.

Adinkra Codes are essentially a set of symbols and images which can be used to represent different ideas. They are often used to express complex ideas and beliefs, such as spiritual teachings and moral principles. The symbols can also be used to represent things such as family history, or stories of achievements.

The Adinkra Codes are used to express an idea or concept in a concise way. For example, the Adinkra symbol of a tortoise can be used to represent patience and perseverance, while a spider symbol can be used to represent strength and resilience.

Adinkra Codes can also be used to create a matrix of symbols and images. This matrix can represent complex ideas and beliefs in a visual way, making it easier for people to understand and relate to them.

Adinkra Codes are an important part of many cultures around the world and are becoming increasingly popular in the modern world. They are a powerful way to communicate complex ideas and to express emotions in a way that everyone can understand. As we continue to live in this MATRIX written on mathematics called ADINKRA CODES, we must remember to appreciate and embrace this unique form of expression.

Functional arrow of time:

Time is a mysterious concept that has been debated for centuries. While the existence of clocks is undeniable, the concept of time itself is much more difficult to pinpoint. In fact, recent discoveries in quantum physics and theoretical physics have led some to suggest that time is an illusion. This concept is known as the "functional arrow of time", which states that time is merely a tool to measure the progress of events. This means that time itself does not move forward or backward, but only provides a way to measure how events are unfolding. This concept has been explored by many scientists and philosophers, however, it still remains a mystery. Ultimately, the true nature of time may never be fully understood, but it is certain that it plays an important role in our lives.

The functional arrow of time allows us to organize our days, weeks, and years in a structured way. We can plan what we need to do, where we need to be, and whom we need to meet up with. This structure helps us to coordinate and collaborate with each other more effectively. It is the foundation of how we plan and structure our lives, allowing us to build and achieve our goals. Without it, we would be lost in a chaotic and unpredictable world.

Time is an interesting concept. It is often thought of as a tangible concept, like a ruler to measure the passing of seconds, minutes, and hours. However, if we take a closer look, time is an illusion. We can use this understanding of time as a tool to master it, and in turn, maximize our potential on this planet.

At the most basic level, we exist in the third dimension. If we were to draw a line on a piece of paper, that would represent the first dimension. In order to move up in the higher dimensions, we must have a greater understanding of time and how to use it. We can use our understanding of the illusion of time to make the most of our lives and ascend to the highest level of existence.

The 4th dimension is something that is often talked about but not always fully understood. At its core, the 4th dimension is a concept that describes time as the 4th dimension of our universe, in addition to the three spatial dimensions. In other words, the 4th dimension allows us to move through time as well as through space. This is a concept that is fairly easy to understand when we look at it as a two-dimensional example. If you draw lines on a piece of paper, you can connect those lines and create a house. This two-dimensional structure is what we see in a computer, although it appears 3-dimensional, it is actually two-dimensional. We, however, exist in the third dimension and can thus see down to the two dimensions and even further down to the one dimension. We have the capability to manipulate these dimensions in order to gain a greater understanding of the world around us and of our higher selves.

The fourth, fifth, and sixth dimensions are inhabited by mysterious beings who exist beyond our own understanding. They exist above us, able to look down into the third dimension and observe us from a higher perspective. From this elevated vantage point, they can witness the past, present, and future all at once, simultaneously. This means that, as far as they are concerned, there is no separation between the different points in time, as the concept of linear time is not applicable to their own reality. Rather than being bound by the same constraints of time and space that govern our existence, these higher dimensional beings can perceive the entirety of existence at once and thus have no need for the concept of an arrow of time.

The fourth dimension is something that has been explored for centuries, as it was first mentioned in ancient texts. This fourth dimension is known as a tesseract, or a quasi-crystal, which is a mathematical structure that is self-similar in all directions. This quasi-crystal contains a repeating pattern that extends in four-dimensional space. This fourth dimension is known as Metatron's cube and it is believed to be the most powerful structure in existence. It is believed that this structure contains divine knowledge that can be used to access higher spiritual realities. The power of this fourth dimension is believed to be so great that it can be used to access divine knowledge and bring about transformation in the physical world. This quasi-crystal has the ability to take us beyond the boundaries of the physical world and into the realm of higher knowledge. By exploring this fourth dimension, we can gain insight into the hidden mysteries of the universe.

Quasi-crystals represent the fourth dimension, casting a shadow that creates the realm in which we exist. This realm is a shadow of a higher dimension, producing a fractal holographic matrix that can be navigated in the third dimension. This matrix provides the foundation for our reality, allowing us to move through its structure and explore the realms of possibility. This is the world we inhabit, a world of shadows and fractals, a world that tilts and shifts depending on our perspective. This is the world of the fourth dimension, a world of quasi-crystals and infinite potential.

As human beings, we are limited to only seeing one percent of the light spectrum. We cannot see gamma rays or ultraviolet light. Yet, we have the power of thought that allows us to travel through light. By using our minds, we are able to connect to other realms and dimensions. Through conscious thought, we can quantum entangle our light waves, allowing us to traverse through time and space. Our minds, combined with light, have the power to show us the universe's limitless possibilities.

In Quantum Physics

Albert Einstein once said that if we consider a third plus a fourth dimension, we can address a fourth dimension of time. However, quantum physics has now revealed that there is actually a fourth dimension, and all dimensions exist at 90-degree angles to each other. This means that when we look at the universe, there are four distinct dimensions that are essential components of our reality.

The fourth dimension of time is an incredibly powerful concept, as it helps us to understand the universe in a more holistic way. We can now look at events that occur in the past, present, and future in relation to one another, and use this knowledge to gain deeper insights and understanding. This could be useful when predicting the outcomes of certain events, or to gain a better understanding of how our universe works.

In conclusion, quantum physics has opened our eyes to the existence of a fourth dimension of time, which has profound implications for our understanding of the universe. With this knowledge, we can gain a deeper understanding of our reality, and use this to make more informed decisions in the future.

Quantum theory has revealed that the universe in which we live is composed of 11 dimensions. This theory has been supported by numerous ancient texts from various civilizations. These texts, from Papyruses to cuneiform tablets, discuss beings that live beyond the known three dimensions of time, space, and matter. It is believed that if there were not at least 11 dimensions, the universe would collapse in on itself. This is why we are eagerly anticipating the discoveries of the additional dimensions. It would open up a whole new realm of understanding and exploration.

It is often speculated that otherworldly beings that visit us from other planets are not just from other galaxies, but in fact, resemble us in many ways. These beings are not exact clones of us, but, rather, are bilateral bipedal hominids that are able to move and manipulate the environment. This is necessary in order to travel through space and other dimensions. In other words, if we were to encounter a being from a distant planet, they would likely be able to speak with us and interact with us in ways that are similar to us.

In recent years, physicists have gained a greater understanding of multi-dimensional beings. This understanding has been aided by advances in quantum physics, which has allowed researchers to analyze and discover the existence of multiple dimensions. These dimensions are so tightly interwoven that if one's atomic structure is shifted; their subatomic frequency is capable of moving into other dimensions.

The implications of this discovery are immense. It could mean that human

beings are capable of accessing realms of existence that were previously thought to be outside of our reach. It could also mean that we are able to understand more about the universe and how it works, as well as the various life forms that inhabit it.

The possibilities of multi-dimensional beings are endless. For example, they could provide us with insights into the nature of the universe, or help us to gain a better understanding of the laws of physics. They could also provide an avenue for scientific exploration and experimentation that could lead to new advancements in technology.

The study of multi-dimensional beings is still in its infancy. But as our understanding of quantum physics continues to evolve, we may find new ways to explore and interact with these mysterious entities. This could open up a whole new world of possibilities, and ultimately help us to understand the universe in ways that were previously unimaginable.

The idea of higher dimensions and their possible connection to paranormal phenomena has long been postulated. People have wondered if these apparitions and paranormal events are a glimpse of something from beyond our universe, from some higher dimension. It is based on research people believe there may be living beings in these higher dimensions. This idea has sparked a great deal of theorizing and speculation about the possibilities. It is an intriguing notion and one that will likely be the source of much debate and investigation for years to come.

Serious Star System

Throughout the vastness of space, there are those living in the third dimension and beyond. Though they may not have physical bodies, their consciousness and knowledge of the universe remain. It is believed that those who reside at a higher level have access to knowledge and understanding that no ordinary being can comprehend. This knowledge and understanding is the Serious Star System, an entity that is unfathomable and yet still exists. It is believed that the Serious Star System holds secrets and answers to questions that have yet to be answered. Those who have access to the knowledge of this system may be able to gain insight into the universe and its many wonders. Perhaps one day, we too can understand the Serious Star System and unlock its secrets

They are connected to a more serious star system that allows them to comprehend the mysteries of the universe and the true power of their own minds. This system operates on a higher frequency and is far more powerful than anything we experience in the third dimension. Through this system, they can gain insight into the greater purpose of their existence and the divine nature of their souls.

The knowledge and wisdom gained from this system can be used to create a better life for oneself, as well as for those around them. They can use this new understanding to bring love, peace, and harmony into their lives, as well as the lives of those around them. Ultimately, this system allows them to reach their highest potential and live a life of joy and abundance.

This is an incredible power that these people have access to, and I believe that it is something we should all strive for. We should all strive to better understand our place in the universe and use this knowledge to create a better future for ourselves and our world.

Sirius is a trinary star system, comprised of stars A, B, and C. Star B is a white dwarf, meaning that it has run out of fuel and is no longer active. This system is of particular interest to the Dogon people, who believe that the star system was taught to them by the Nomo. According to their beliefs, the Nomo shared knowledge about the star's orbital patterns, as well as our entire solar system, including its shape, names, sizes, and colors. This knowledge has been passed down through generations and continues to be a source of intrigue and wonder.

The nomo taught them all the planets in our solar system: Mercury, Venus, Earth, Mars, Jupiter, Saturn, Uranus, Neptune, and Pluto. They even knew the planetary alignments: when two or more planets appear close together in the sky. Furthermore, they even knew about the white dwarf star, which is so gravitationally heavy that one spoonful couldn't be left by over one million men. They even knew the immense gravity of this star and the amazing fact that a spoonful of it was too heavy for a million men to lift. Such knowledge was truly incredible and it speaks to the high intelligence of the nomo.

Error Correcting Codes

rediscovered the star and then was able to turn it into a three-dimensional object. After that, he discovered error-correcting codes while analyzing the star. Error-correcting codes are essential in quantum physics, and Professor Gates' discovery was very important in furthering understanding and knowledge of the field.

Professor James Gates was in the midst of analyzing error-correcting codes when he made an incredible discovery. He found that the entire ether of space-time, in other words, all of the matter and energy that makes up the universe, was operating on a specific code. This code, which has been dubbed the Dinker code, is believed to be responsible for allowing information to be accessed throughout the entire universe. This groundbreaking discovery has the potential to revolutionize the way we understand the universe and its operations.

Error-correcting codes are a type of Dinker code that allow search engines, web browsers, and other technologies to run as smoothly as possible. What many people don't realize is that everything in the third dimension is based on life, so in essence, we are all made of light. This means that even this avatar body, this chair, and this table are all made of slowed-down light waves. This is an incredible concept and one that helps us to understand the universe a little better.

Solid Matter

This chair we are sitting on, the table you are sitting at, and the avatar body - what is this? This actually slowed down light waves. When light is slowed down and consciousness interacts with it, it collapses into what we call solid matter. So, solid matter is actually an illusion - for example, the only thing stopping my hand from going through this chair is the repulsion of electromagnetism. This is how we are able to interact with the physical world.

If I can phase shift the atomic frequency of my hand to match the same frequency of the atoms in this chair, I would be able to pass my hand right through it. This is because atoms are composed of 99.999% empty space. That means we, too, are a fractal of empty space, yet we are conscious and the consciousness is formed by light. We are conscious beings of light, and that is why we are able to exist.

Fractal

It is amazing to think that if you were to look at a hologram, no matter how small the piece you may look at, you will still be able to see the entire image in that smallest piece. Of course, you may sacrifice a bit of resolution, but it is still incredible to think of the power of fractals. When we look at the universe it is like a fractal, and when we look at our consciousness it is also like a fractal. In a way, our consciousness is a fractal of the universe, and understanding this helps us to better understand our place in the cosmos. Ultimately, we are all part of this incredible fractal, and it is important to remember this.

It is truly incredible to think that each and every thought that we think actually leaves our minds in the form of a light wave. This phenomenon has been studied in scientific experiments, where researchers have used a cap with electrodes to measure brain activity as people think. The results of these experiments show up on a computer screen, and they provide an amazing insight into the power of our minds and consciousness. This knowledge is further revealed through studying fractal patterns, which allow us to study the complex interconnections between the elements of consciousness. This understanding of the intricate relationship between our thoughts and the universe around us is truly remarkable, and it is an incredible privilege to be a part of it.

Quantum-entangling

This phenomenon of quantum entangling with someone on the other side of the universe is becoming more and more accepted by mainstream quantum physicists and theoretical physicists. The idea is that in some cases, we are able to access information or ideas that we didn't consciously come up with. This is because our minds have become entangled with information from the other side, allowing us to download this information and ideas. This phenomenon proves how powerful and infinite the power of the universe can be.

Light

We all have the power to transmit energy, whether it is positive or negative. When someone is at a low frequency, we can enter the room with a high frequency and our light being can raise their energy level. However, if we are not high enough and they are already low, our energy can drop theirs. This energy exchange is also connected to our conscious power and strength. We can also interact with and exchange information with the entire multiverse. This is truly a remarkable ability that we have to connect and share with those around us.

The potential of being able to discern information and put action behind it is one of the greatest inventions of our time. Web 3, Non-Fungible Tokens, and other inventions have the potential to revolutionize our society. However, there is a dark side to this technological progress - the emasculation of men in our society. This emasculation is, in many cases, driven by chemical castration, a form of chemical manipulation. Microplastics, specifically, have been identified as a major contributor to the problem, and their presence in the environment is something that needs to be addressed in order to prevent further degradation of the male gender. With the right steps, we can create a society that is able to reap the benefits of technological advances, without sacrificing the well-being of our citizens.

Micro-plastics

The recent test on micro-plastics has revealed some disturbing results. It was found that frogs were being converted from male to female due to the ingestion of these particles. Furthermore, the levels of testosterone in men have been recorded to be the lowest they have ever been. This means that the ability of people to make logical decisions is also dropping. This is a worrying sign for our society, as it indicates that the environment is having a negative impact on our health and well-being. We must act to reduce our exposure to microplastics and other pollutants in order to protect ourselves and future generations.

7

Chapter Seven

The Hermetic Principles: The Seven Principles

"If knowledge is not put into practice, it does not benefit one."
Muhammad Tahir-ul-Qadri

The seven principles are the foundation of Hermeticism, a branch of spiritual philosophy dating back over 5000 years ago. They were outlined by famed author Hermes Trismegistus (mean to be born 3 times), who is believed to have written the Emerald Tablet and the Corpus Hermeticum (two highly influential, ancient teachings). His work would go on to influence both ancient Greek and Egyptian cultures, with both adopting him as a god of wisdom. (In Greece he was called Hermes; in Egypt, Thoth.) He was known in his time as a great master of the universe and is said to have lived for thousands of years.

Over time, the seven hermetic principles were passed down by word-of-mouth from teacher to student, and eventually, one day in the early 20th century, the teachings were compiled into a book called The Kybalion, written by "The Three Initiates." Today, they remain an occult source of wisdom, separate from any real religion but powerful nonetheless. And while the seven principles are just one way of understanding the universe, they aren't so constricting that they cannot be studied alongside other spiritual philosophies.

First. We have the **law of mentalism** then the **law of Correspondence** then the **law of vibration** then the **law of polarity** after that we **have the law of rhythm cause and effect and gender**

The Law of Mentalism states that the mind is the one true reality and that all physical forms found in the universe are simply manifestations of the mental plane. The Law of Correspondence follows, stating that there is a close connection between the physical and mental realms and that what is found in one is echoed in the other. The Law of Vibration postulates that all matter is in constant motion and that the higher the vibration, the more powerful the energy is. This is followed by the Law of Polarity, which states that every force has an opposite and that these two opposing forces are interconnected and interdependent in nature. Lastly, we have the Law of Rhythm, Cause and Effect, and Gender, which states that all matter is subject to the same natural laws and that the action of one force upon another result in a certain effect.

Principle of Mentalism:

The principle of mentalism; is that all is mind, and the universe is mental, this principle embodies the truth that all is mind it explains that all which is the substantial reality underlying all outward manifestations and appearances which we call the material universe is in short spirit and spirit although undefinable is likened unto the infinite living mind

for Mind and Spirit are truly one and the same interchangeable terms to the Hermetic being aware of this first Universal principle of mentalism can directly improve our lives by understanding that before anything gets drawn into the manifested physical outward world it is first harnessed through the creative intelligence of the energy that we know as the mind so applying our mental faculties to our Creations is how we first draw them into the physical world.

Principle of Correspondence:

The principle of Correspondence, As Above So Below as within so without as the universe so the soul the truth that is embodied within this principle is that there is always a correspondence between the laws and the phenomena of the various planes of being and life, the old hermetic Axiom ran in these words as above so below as below so above and the grasping of this principle gives one of the means of solving many a dark Paradox, now, I personally find this law to be the most helpful when seeking Clarity because what it is saying is that by us knowing our own Nature by us knowing our own mind and by us knowing the world around us it is reflecting what is happening and taking place in the worlds and the planes of Consciousness above us so the more we study the below we are able to understand and comprehend the above this is vital to be aware of as a seeker of truth because now we are able to tell what's happening in the cosmos and what's taking place in the higher planes of Consciousness by simply observing the world around us and most importantly our internal landscape.

The Principle of Vibration

The principle of vibration nothing rests everything moves everything vibrates. This principle embodies the truth that everything is in motion everything vibrates and nothing is ever truly at rest this principle explains that the differences between different manifestations of matter, energy, mind, and even Spirit result largely just from varying rates of vibration it has been said that one who truly understands this law of vibration is one who has grasped the scepter of power because within this law we are able to understand that everything in existence is expressed through vibration and that there are just simply different rates of vibration and within these different rates of vibration are entirely different Realms of experience and of creation so when we know that all is truly vibration then we also know that by raising the vibration of our Consciousness that now we unlock access to the manifestations that we wish to create which are vibrating at that level of reality.

The principle of polarity: everything is dual everything has pulls everything has its

The principle of Polarity pair of opposites like and unlike are the same opposites that are identical in nature but different in degree extremes meet all truths are but half-truths all paradoxes may be reconciled this principle embodies the truth that everything is dual everything has two poles everything has its pair of opposites all of which were old hermetic axioms everything is and is not at the same time all truths are but half-truths every truth is half false there are two sides of everything,

it explains that in everything there are two poles or opposite aspects and that opposites are really only the two extremes of the same thing the example the Kybalion gives us is that there is no such thing as absolute heat or absolute cold the two terms heat and cold simply indicate varying degrees of the same thing and that same thing which manifests as heat and cold is merely a form a rate of vibration so heat and cold are simply the two poles of that which we call Heat the same principle manifests in the case of light and darkness which are the same thing the difference consisting of varying degrees between these two poles of the same phenomena so what you really have is the absence of light or the presence of light and when there is an absence of light that is what we call Darkness although they are just two poles of that one thing that one phenomenon.

This law of polarity can best improve our lives by giving us the clarity to view the world around us how many times have we seen opposing forces act identically in nature how many times have we loved so much that it turned into its polar opposite hate and how many times have we cared so much that it traveled all the way over to its polar opposite numbness these are all different examples of the law of polarity and how one energy gets split into Polar Opposites along a spectrum.

The principle of rhythm:

Everything flows out and in everything has its tides all things rise and fall the pendulum swing manifests in everything the measure of the swing to the right is the measure of the swing to the left rhythm compensates this principle embodies the truth that in everything there is manifested a measured motion to and from a flow and inflow a swing backward and forward a pendulum-like movement this law is so important because when we are interpreting what we see inside this age if we don't have knowledge of the law of Rhythm we won't understand that this is actually a Redemption Arc there is some sort of return that is happening meaning that if there was ever a group of people or let's just call it a movement some sort of thought form even if it's ancient knowledge whatever it is that was once suppressed, it will now come in to its complete opposite its hero Redemption Arc, so when we are using the law of Rhythm we are actually understanding the larger context of what's Happening inside this age because we're viewing it now through its proper lens we can better understand that all of the overarching themes that we see taking place within this age are actually coming from a larger cycle when we possess the knowledge of this law of Rhythm we are able to perceive an inevitable pendulum-like swing that takes place within movements and within consciousness and however strong of a degree that was pushed to one side of the pendulum will be the exact intensity that that pendulum swing carries out to its opposite knowing this is how the Alchemists extract themselves from this momentum of karma and then we consciously position ourselves wherever we want to in this pendulum swing and by consciously choosing our position there then we neutralize ourselves there and that's how we avoid the karmic momentum that's taking place to and from the cycles of nature.

Principle of Cause and Effect

The principle of cause and effect every cause has its effect every effect has its cause everything happens according to law chances but a name for law not recognized there are many planes of causation but nothing escapes the law this principle embodies the fact that there is a cause for every effect and an effect for every cause it explains that everything happens according to law and that nothing is ever merely by chance this love cause and effect goes by an even more popular term known as karma and what this law also contains within it is the knowledge that Karma can reside on higher planes of Consciousness which means that the cause of whatever we're experiencing as the effect is not always coming from the material realm knowing that there is always a cause and an effect at play can vastly improve our lives if we use that knowledge the way that the ancient Alchemist did by Shifting the way that we are affected by that cause when we shift the way that we react to any response or stimulus now we are able to transcend that karmic thread this is first done by doing our best to understand what originated that cause what was the first action that caused that reaction and then from there choosing with our own conscious free will to respond in a different manner rather than react from an automated state of unconsciousness.

The Alchemist applies their own Consciousness and their own free will in order to shift cause from effect and to shift the effect from its cause.

Principle of Gender

The principle of gender states that gender isn't everything has its masculine and feminine principles gender manifests on all planes this principle embodies the truth that there is gender manifested in everything on the physical plane the principle manifests as sex on the higher planes it takes higher forms but the principle is always the same everything and every person contains the two elements every male thing has the female element within it and every female thing contains the male element within it, the principle of gender is profoundly valuable because once we understand that we contain both masculine and feminine elements to varying degrees and ratios we can use that for mental creation the same way on the physical plane that the masculine and feminine energies create life on the mental plane we can use our masculine and feminine energies and the elements within us to create and to regenerate we can apply this law to our mental Creations by drawing them towards us with our magnetism our magnetism is a part of our emotional body and the emotional body

is our feminine elements so when we combined our masculine energies such as thought and action with our feminine energies of magnetism coming from the emotional body and the emotional experience that we're calling forward through the sensations of our emotions what we're doing is amplifying our ability to be magnetic and just like a magnet our Creations get drawn forward and called to us so unifying these two energies is how we call forward our manifestations now what I'm about to tell you about these seven hermetic principles has never been taught anywhere before it has never been written of and it has never been told and that is these seven laws are actually one principle and one law that gets emanated into seven different rays and into seven different laws and principles so they're actually all the same law and the reason we see them as seven is because there are seven different expressions and ways that they are conveyed you will most likely have to meditate upon what I have just said in order to deeply and truly understand it I recommend that you recognize these laws for yourself don't take my word for it go out into your lives and notice how these seven principles play out and interact with one another in everything small or large within or without.

8

Chapter Eight

" You are not a drop in the ocean; You are the entire ocean in a drop."
- Rumi

The Divine Power of Water

Dynamic water, when it is alive and energized, performs the role of initiating and operating all the processes of life. The most important function of biological water is to facilitate rapid inter-communication between cells and connective tissues so that the organism can function as a coordinated whole. Though not recognized by mainstream science, living water in fact performs this intercommunication function between all organisms and even between life on Earth and the Cosmos, so that nothing can happen without affecting the other.

We are deeply connected with water and it is a part of us and our lives. On a sunny spring day, we can feel the energy of the water rising and rejuvenating us. The sun's warmth and the water's life-giving energy combine to create a feeling of joy and vitality. The sound of a waterfall or the sound of the ocean can also bring us a feeling of peace and calm. Water has the power to evoke strong emotions, whether it is the splash of a cool river on a hot summer day or the sight of a placid lake on a misty morning. Water has a deep, primordial connection to us and our lives, and we can use it to help us relax, refresh and re-energize.

Humans have always had an intimate relationship with water. Its power to create and destroy has been seen as essential to life and its importance in our lives is undeniable. Water has been incorporated into many of the world's most ancient and powerful religions, and its significance and symbolism have been celebrated for centuries.

Water has a unique power to soothe and energize us, to inspire and to heal. It is the source of life, but also a reminder of our mortality and of the fragility of our existence. It can link us to our past, to our present, and to our future. Water is a living, breathing thing that has the capacity to bring us together and help us understand our place in the world.

The power of water is seen in its ability to move us, to give us hope, and to remind us of the beauty of life. It is a source of strength and resilience, and a reminder of our interconnectedness with the environment and with each other. Water resonates deeply with humans and its presence in our lives is undeniable.

Water carries all life. But water is beyond time, for it bears in its flow the seeds of future life, as well as the memory of past life. Water mediates between life and death, between being and not being, and between health and sickness. We have lost touch with the magic of water, the freshness of the mountain spring, the reflection in a mountain lake, and the mystery of the sacred well. We just take for granted that water will come at the turn of a tap.

We have allowed water to spread illness and disease. Much is spoken about these days of the destructive nature of water. Such water is Nature on the rampage, perhaps showing who is boss, at a time when humanity has wrought so much reckless damage to Earth's ecosystems and to the natural environment.

Our bodies are composed of about 70% water, a similar percentage to that of the ocean surface compared to land. Blood and sap are really variations of water. Earth is known as the planet of water; astronauts wondered at Earth's blue, shimmering, watery aura seen from space. It seems as if water was intended for life; certainly, life could not have come without it. Water is found throughout the Universe, though seldom as a liquid, which requires the relatively narrow temperature band that our Earth provides.

Without a doubt, water is the most important substance on Earth. It drives everything, from the most delicate metabolic processes in our bodies to creating environments favourable to life, to weather patterns and climate change.

The poet, philosopher, and scientist, Johann Wolfgang von Goethe (1749-1832) was, more than anyone, a bridge between pre-and post-Enlightenment thinking. He sensed a profound difference in outlook between the new rational, mechanistic, and more exclusive worldview, and the more traditional inclusive, Nature-centred view. He called the latter 'holistic' science in contrast to 'reductionist' science. Goethe understood that all life is one, closely interconnected and interrelated, with water as the very symbol of holism, with its role in the sustenance of life.

Goethe referred to water as "the ground of all being." Thales of Miletus (640-546 BCE) also believed water to be infused with Being, believing it was the original substance of the Cosmos. The Austrian 'Water Wizard', Viktor Schauberger (1885-1958), held a similar view, saying that water is the product of the subtle energies that brought the Earth into being and is itself a living substance.

Sacred Knowledge

Water has always been revered and respected, from antiquity to the present day. Until recently, it took a great deal of effort and labour to collect water for domestic use, with many places around the world still requiring this effort today. Water was seen as a divine resource, believed to be protected and blessed by gods. This was due to its vital importance for life, both for humans and other creatures, and its scarcity in some parts of the world. Ancient cultures would have elaborate ceremonies and rituals to honour this life-giving resource, and many cultures today still consider water a sacred element. It is no wonder that water has been treated with reverence throughout history, due to its sheer importance and its limited availability in certain areas.

One of the principal cultural ceremonies of the Pacific Northwest indigenous tribes in British Columbia was the 'potlatch', believed to have been practiced for thousands of years. Usually, a part of this complex ceremony was given to the recitation of the spiritual traditions of the tribe. The 'speaker', a position often handed down in one of the chief families, performed this important role.

The training of future speakers was a long-observed ritual, involving teaching the young person to listen to the wind from mountaintops, to the sound of the ocean waves on the rocky shore, and to the music of the rushing stream. This was done to encourage the young person to incorporate Nature's sounds and cadences into their stories and to develop an appreciation for the wisdom of the tribe. Water was particularly sacred to these people, as it was regarded as a medium of communication with the gods. Listening to the sounds of the water was believed to provide insight into the unknown. As part of their training, the young speaker would often take part in rituals at the river or sea, absorbing the sound of the water to help them gain a deeper understanding of the stories they were told. By connecting with the natural world, they could come to appreciate the importance of wisdom passed down throughout the generations. In this way, they could ensure that the stories they told would live on.

Water has long been an influential force in the development of language and writing. This can be seen in many ancient scripts, which use flowing lines similar to water in their characters, such as Hebrew. Greek writing further developed this concept, but it was Latin that broke the cycle and its angular, straight characters that moved away from the influence of water. Latin script became the foundation of Euclidean geometry, featuring circles, straight lines, and points. This was a major departure from Nature and natural forms. The estrangement from Nature created by Latin script has been echoed in the development of language, particularly in the West, where Latin-based language has become the dominant force. This shift has had a lasting impact on language, with water no longer informing the writing process as it did in the past.

Nostradamus' use of water as a scrying tool is just one of the many esoteric uses for water. Indeed, its spiritual power has been recognized for centuries and its ability to provide insight into the future has been long-acknowledged. But it is not only in these spiritual uses that water is powerful. Viktor Schauberger, a pioneering researcher in the field of hydrodynamics, had a remarkable experience while listening to the music of a rushing stream in his Alpine refuge. He had a profound intuition that water needs to be handled and moved in a certain way to remain healthy and vital. This intuition was to inform his groundbreaking research and lead to many of his discoveries. His work on the behavior of water has had a great influence on modern hydrodynamics and continues to be studied today.

Water is truly a mysterious and powerful element, with many uses, both esoteric and practical.

In recent centuries, our attitude towards water has shifted drastically. We have become ever more disconnected from the true power of water as we have embraced the rise of rationalism and denied the spiritual influences of humanity over Nature. In our pursuit of technological progress and the declaration of human supremacy over Nature, we have lost sight of the magical qualities of water. We no longer recognize the essential role that water plays in our lives, and we have become so focused on our own laws and regulations that we have failed to appreciate the importance of water for our planet.

Our understanding of water has been shaped by our own beliefs and assumptions, and our neglect of its spiritual properties has resulted in us taking it for granted. We have failed to recognize the integral role of water in sustaining life, and our overuse and misuse of water have had devastating repercussions on our environment. We need to return to a reverence for water and its power and develop an appreciation for its spiritual and physical properties. Only then can we begin to restore the balance of Nature and once again appreciate the beauty and magic of water.

Water is much more than just an inorganic compound, as our biology and physics textbooks would lead us to believe. In fact, many ancient cultures had a deeper understanding of water, recognizing its special qualities. This is likely due to the fact that they did not have the same limited worldview that mainstream science has today. This obsession with the physical nature of life means we know very little about the true potential of water and the profound effects it can have on our lives. From providing essential nutrients to sustaining life, water has been a vital part of human existence since the beginning of time. Despite its integral role in our lives, we are only just beginning to uncover its mysteries.

Holism

The key to understanding water and living more in tune with our environment is to learn to see and feel holistically as part of a community of beings – human, animal, microbial, and botanical – united by a common bond of water. It is through the medium of water that we all share a common heritage – we are all One.

Ancient mystical systems, especially Hindu, Taoist, and Buddhist, held water in particular reverence and understood some of its quantum qualities, even if they did not describe them in terms of quantum science. Neils Bohr and Robert Oppenheimer, pioneers of quantum physics, and more recently David Bohm, Einstein's protégé, found remarkable similarities between their new worldview and the concept of the oneness of all creation held by those mystical systems.*1*

Water is the epitome of holism. It connects all of life, and life cannot exist without it. Spiritual and mystical experiences have a strong link with holism.

Dynamic water, when it is alive and energized, performs the role of initiating and operating all the processes of life. The most important function of biological water is to facilitate rapid inter-communication between cells and connective tissues so that the organism can function as a coordinated whole. Though not recognized by mainstream science, living water in fact performs this intercommunication function between all organisms, groups of organisms, populations, natural kingdoms, and the world, creating a network of sensitivity throughout all of life, even between life on Earth and the Cosmos, so that nothing can happen without affecting other processes; all are linked together by water. In this way, it drives evolution.*2*

The story needs to be told simply of how water is the stage manager of life, communicating to our bodies' cells how to be part of a vast orchestra; how it distributes energy to make the landscape balanced and productive. Indeed, the very laws which govern the harmonious movement of the planets also determined the form and behavior of our organic life, through water. This extraordinary picture of water's part in the evolution of life derives from the discovery of the quantum field that interconnects all of creation in a vast web of energy. Rudolf Steiner and his interpreter Theodor Schwenk believed that the quantum field (also known as the etheric field) contains the encoded data bank of the information required for evolution to proceed.

Yin Yang Balance

Viktor Schauberger demonstrated how life, both at the maintenance level and in evolutionary processes depends on the subtle balancing between energy polarities, shown at its best in the unstable balancing between positive and negative polarities in water's behavior. These have not been well described in scientific writing, therefore a summary of their importance would seem desirable.

The Sun is our main source of energy. In Chinese tradition, it emits a positive, *yang* (masculine) energy. The Earth balances this with a *yin*, or feminine (negative) energy. Without this interplay, there would be no water, plants, or chemical compounds. *Yin* and *yang* are dynamic in the sense that their energy fluctuates – when one expands, the other diminishes. The concentration of energy is a *yin* process, while that to move and disperse is a *yang.* Western thought holds them as fixed states, but in the Chinese tradition, they are constantly shifting. Thus, in every man, there is feminine energy and, in every woman, there is masculine energy, these tendencies vary in different situations. It is the same in Nature. Mornings tend to have Y*ang* energy and evenings, Y*in*.

As Fritjof Capra comments: "Chinese sages seem to have recognized the basic polarity that is characteristic of living systems. Self-assertion is achieved by displaying *yang* behavior; by being demanding, aggressive, competitive, expanding, and – as far as human behavior is concerned – by using linear, analytical political thinking.

Integration is furthered by *yin* behavior; by being responsive, cooperative, intuitive, and aware of one's environment. Both *yin* and *yang*, integrative and self-assertive tendencies, are necessary for harmonious social and ecological relationships."*4*

One can see that our society has favored *yang* over *yin* – rational knowledge over intuitive wisdom, science over religion, competition over cooperation, and exploitation over conservation.

All processes depend on an unstable reciprocity between extremes. As soon as a process becomes stable, it stagnates. It's the same with water. Moving, circulating water is energized; still, water is effectively dead. Water is the ideal medium for processes because it is an unstable and dynamic medium, and without water, nothing in Earth's environment can change.

Nature is founded far more on cooperation than on competition because it is only through the harmonious interplay of energy that physical formation can occur and structures can be built up. At the heart of the creative process in Nature are negative and positive polarities, such as chaos and order, quantity and quality, gravitation and levitation, and electricity and magnetism. (The last polarities Schauberger studied as complementary qualities.) In every case, for any natural process to be harmonious, one polarity cannot be present without the other, and each needs the other to make up the whole.

Natural law, as Viktor Schauberger describes, requires that, for creative evolution to be maintained, the polarities are not 50/50, which would result in atrophy, but are unevenly balanced towards the *yin* or negative. Water's principal quality is to bring balance to life. For this reason, you would expect it to be very stable; in fact, the reverse is true. The water molecule is made up of two smalls positively charged hydrogen atoms and one very large negatively charged oxygen atom; the strong bifurcated hydrogen bonds are unsymmetrical, which makes water unstable and unpredictable. This instability belongs not only to the aquatic sphere; it is the guiding law of the Universe since its inception. Instability and unpredictability are the secrets of matter's very existence and the impulse for creativity. As we all know, predictability is the recipe for a boring existence. It is the restlessness of water that stimulates its pulsation and constant swinging between the *yin* and the *yang.*

The dance of creation is the harmonious interplay through the attraction and repulsion of polarised atoms. The mutual attraction of 2x H and 1x O gives birth to the marvel of water. The catalytic role of dual polarity is initiated by the positive charge of the Sun, the inseminator of life, which melds with the Earth's receptive and feminine energy. Together they are essential components for all biological processes.

We don't normally think of water carrying an electric charge, but its bioelectrical sensitivity is one of the most important qualities in its importance for life. The electromagnetic qualities of mineral-rich or saline water allow it to steer processes and evolution by constantly shifting the energy reciprocally between positive and negative charges. Schauberger showed that a natural river flowing sinuously across the landscape recharges its energy towards the positive or *yang* on the right-hand bend and towards the negative or *yin* on the left-hand bend. This constant accumulation of y*in* and *yang* charges raises the energy level of the water so that it can perform its true role in nurturing the landscape. The same happens with our biological water.

Through spiralling movement, water maintains its energy as 'living water'. In its most dynamic state, water develops the structure of a vortex which raises its energy level – more quickly if the direction of the spin alternates between left and right.

Because the quantum or etheric field is universal and water is common in the Universe, associated with life or potential life, it seems natural to view them as complementary, working together. In esoteric terms the etheric (sometimes called "the God field") may be seen as the masculine *(yang)*, *initiating* polarity; while the water medium has the *receptive*, feminine *(yin)* role. What I propose is that the water medium and the quantum field are two complementary aspects in the balanced mediation, sustenance and evolution of life. You might call this a candidate for the 'Unified Field Theory'.

If we say that water builds the physical structures of living organisms, this begs the question of where are the templates. We believe they are held in the etheric or quantum field, often encoded in sacred geometry.*5* For example the indispensable container for the emergence of new life is the egg shape, the only shape in which water can circulate spontaneously: the egg and similar shapes like the pine cone, or spiral structures such as seashells or leaf designs have a symmetry defined by *phi* (Φ) or 'The Golden Section'. These symmetries have a *yin/yang* ratio which can be defined mathematically by the number 1:1.618033988, which seems always to be associated in Nature with the transmutation of energy into form.*6*

Communication

What is the scientific evidence for water as a communication medium? An exciting discovery in recent years has been the strange role that water plays in biological communication. It has come to light that collagen, the connective tissue that makes up the bulk of all multicellular animals, is crucial to the integrity of the organism. It is composed of a crystalline matrix of collagen proteins embedded in water, compromising 60-70% by weight. This water is specially structured in chains along the collagen fibers and has the ability to self-organize.

Dr Mae-Wan Ho, the co-founder of the Institute for Science in Society, and one of the most prominent holistic biophysicists has specialized in the role of biological water. She believes that the collagen chains enable water to become superconductive, an ideal medium for instantaneous communication for coordination of all cellular activities. She believes that this liquid crystal continuum constitutes our "body consciousness" that may well have evolved before the nervous system, but which today works both in partnership with, and also independently of, the nervous system.

Sentience is the capacity for conscious experience, and it is derived from a form of body consciousness that involves the integration of the energy storage domain. This domain is composed of the various interrelated parts of a living organism and its environment, and it is responsible for the ability of the organism to understand and process information. Without this intercommunicating whole of the energy storage domain, sentience would not be possible. Therefore, it can be said that this body consciousness is the basis of sentience, the prerequisite for conscious experience.

We hear increasingly of water being described as a "conscious organism." It is an organism in the sense that it has integrity, independence, cohesion, and particular qualities that allow it to be the driver of life and evolution. The quality of consciousness may also seem a strange term to apply to water. But if it's the medium of communication, it could also be the medium of consciousness. Viktor Schauberger and Theodor Schwenk demonstrated that the water medium also has intelligence. Water has the quality of restlessness which gives living systems the ability to become ever more complex and to strive forward toward perfection.

We use the term 'intelligence' in connection with water because it optimizes the conditions for life by regulating environmental processes. At a temperature of 37°C (98.4°F), water requires a very large input or removal of kinetic energy in order for its temperature to rise, allowing it to keep the blood in the human body at a constant temperature of 37°C, any deviation from which indicates illness. Another of the intelligence of water is that it takes a lot of energy to freeze and, once frozen to melt; and a huge amount of energy to vaporize water which stops the air from excessive heating. This makes water a very effective balancer against climatic extremes. The warmer the air, the more water vapor it can hold, and the longer the temperature can remain constant.

The interaction of these three properties of water has created a temperate climate zone on Earth with optimum conditions for the evolution of the human species. Certainly, complex civilizations could not have evolved without the stability of moderate, stable climates. Without these self-regulating systems, life could never have developed beyond the simplest forms.

Water's Memory

Much has been written about water's memory. Does it have a memory? Masaru Emoto studied the structure of ice crystals to determine the quality of their liquid water origin. He demonstrates how poor-quality water cannot build good structures, while high-quality water produces the most beautiful crystalline designs. Amazingly, water that has been exposed to harmonious music or exalted human energies can produce pure beautiful crystals, while when it is exposed to disruptive energies it cannot produce well-structured crystals.

When water is flowing as its nature dictates, energetically in spirals and vortices, and continually changing its state, the molecules, if conditions permit, organize themselves into structures, layers, or clusters of vibrating energy centers that carry constructive information, constantly receiving and transmitting energy from every contact the water body makes.

These clusters or layers can store vibrational energy impressions or imprints, rather like magnetic tape. If these are beneficial, they may be able to restore healthy resonance in the human body, as in homeopathy. On the other hand, if there are imprints of toxins or pollutants in the drinking water, they may be carriers of disharmony and disease.

Water does have a memory. When we think we have 'purified' water of the chemicals and hormones we have mindlessly thrown in, in order to make it drinkable, the energy of these contaminants remains, polluting our energy bodies in the same way that chemicals affect our physical bodies. Because of its nature, water sacrifices itself entirely to the environment, for good or for bad.

Experiencing the spiritual qualities of water can be an incredibly profound and powerful experience. For us, it came spontaneously when we realized that we are embedded in the infinite continuum of water that contains all living creatures. This realization was much more powerful than simply having the intellectual idea of being connected to one another, and it helped us to understand the concept of "we are all one" through the interconnectedness of water.

Through this realization, we began to appreciate the beauty and power of water in a way that goes beyond its physical properties. We have come to understand that water is a source of energy, life, and healing, and that it serves as an integral part of our spiritual selves. We use the energy of water to cleanse and purify our minds, bodies, and spirits, and we can use it to heal ourselves and others. We can also use it to spiritually connect with the world around us and to gain insight into our lives.

To experience the spiritual qualities of water, we suggest starting with simple activities. Spend a few moments outside, near a body of water such as a river or a lake, and simply observe the movement of the water. Feel the energy and power of the water, and be mindful of how it connects you to the rest of the world. You can also practice meditating near a body of water, or you can even practice meditation while immersed in water. By connecting with the spiritual energy of water, you can open yourself up to a whole new level of understanding and appreciation of the world around you.

In Eastern tradition, greeting someone is a way of showing humility, respect, and recognition of their Divine nature. It is a gesture of reverence and gratitude to the other person and a way of acknowledging their unique place in the universe. When greeting someone in this way, one typically bows their head or places their palms together in front of their heart. This gesture acknowledges the other person's Divine nature and the sacred link that our biological water, or blood, has to the Divine in all of us. Thus, when we greet someone in this way, we are connecting to something greater than ourselves and recognizing the importance of their presence in the world.

9

Chapter Nine

THE PYRAMID CODE

"All of nature begins to whisper its secrets to us through its sounds. Sounds that were previously incomprehensible to our soul now become the meaningful language of nature."

MYSTICISM OF THE PYRAMID:

The Pyramids are a mysterious and powerful relic of ancient history. They have long mystified researchers and historians alike, with their seemingly impossible construction, and their secrets have yet to be fully revealed.

What is known is that these ancient structures are constructed in such a way that they are able to respond to the gravitational pull of the star or planet in which they are located. This enables the ancient tools and instruments to work and move in response to the pull of gravity.

Gravity is the force that binds all material on Earth together, drawing it back to our planet's core. It symbolizes and expresses the connection between creation and nature, a bond that is guided by divine power. We must always strive to work with gravity and not against it, as going against it leads to failure.

This is true no matter what we are constructing, be it a pyramid or a temple – if we try to go against gravity, everything will eventually come crashing down. Working in harmony with gravity is the only way to ensure success in our endeavors.

In addition to this, there is also the idea that the Pyramids represent our own self-consciousness. This is based on the idea that the structure of the Pyramids reflects the same principles that govern the human mind. It is said that by studying the Pyramids, we can gain a deeper understanding of our own consciousness.

The Pyramids and the secrets they contain are an incredible legacy of ancient civilizations. They are a testament to the power of the human mind to construct wonders that respond to the laws of nature and to our own innermost thoughts. They are a reminder of our own potential to reach greatness, and to be inspired by the mysteries of the past.

The Pyramids were constructed by and according to the laws of nature and in accordance with various mathematical, physical, astronomical, and astrological laws. In the Pharaonic era, astronomy and astrology were considered as one science or knowledge and were called "ast" in the Fatasol language. Every minor or High Priest had to be proficient in "ast" sciences. The Pyramid is to be used for a number of purposes: protection, an eternal clock, an eternal calendar, and a tomb for the Fatasol. The Pyramids were used as tombs for the purpose of using the Divine bodies of the Fatasol Beings as an energetic defense for the Pyramid, its entrances, and the instruments that exist within it. Pharaoh and the High Priest had an energy within their bodies that is also present after they die which acts as a protection for the doors and gates of the Pyramid. They were intended to be the gatekeepers through the use of their internal energy and through preserving their bodies after they died. Normal human beings do not understand this energy because they cannot measure it. However, the supreme goal of the Pyramid was protection. Every Pyramid was carefully designed and built. Its location, angle, size of each rock and type of rock all had a specific reason. For example, the angles of the walls relative to their bases were built at 51 degrees for various reasons, one of which was to have the sun's rays reflected great distances. The Pyramid also served as a lighthouse for both humans and spaceships during the day and at night. Laser beams projected from the apex of the Pyramid towards the sky, also at a specific angle to specific stars in order to be in constant communication with different motherships and different stars (planets) that may, over the years, become a new home just as the Earth became a new home for the Fatasol beings in the year 1010 according to the Hebrew calendar (2750 BC according to the Gregorian calendar). Originally, all the pyramids were facing different directions according to the stars that they communicated with. However, for reasons unknown, most of the Pyramids on Earth and every Pyramid on any other planet or star (probably in the millions) were completely destroyed after the Exodus. As I stated earlier, there are fewer than 100,000 Pyramids left on Earth. All of them are facing North (North Star). There is one star/planet in the physical shape of a Pyramid that rotates (counter-clockwise) and moves constantly in the Heavens for probably eternity. I know today that the Pyramid star/planet is the home of "Adam"

The entire history of the aliens is carved on the walls within the secret rooms, secret tunnels, and secret cellars of the Pyramids. Transcribed on these walls is the history of the Pyramid code as well as the eternal code itself. This infinite knowledge will become common knowledge one day and human beings will be able to read it, understand it, and use it to decipher the past, present, and future that all exist in the present moment. Since God is everywhere and in everything alive (humans and animals), plant life, inanimate and spiritual, we must first understand that a Pyramid or any other structure is part of God. That is, part of the collective spirit. This means that physical structures are also controlled by the laws of the spirit (the mysticism of the spirit). The third-dimensional world is based on the laws of the spirit which we cannot exist without. This means that a Pyramid is as much of the eternal Divine Being as anything else in the universe.

In order to understand these laws, we must first understand God (source), which is not an easy task. God lives in everything and everything lives in God.

God, in “His” perfection, can only be understood by those who can or have become God themselves (10th dimension). To summarize this insight, *only God can understand God.* Since we, as human beings, have been cut off from our Divine-self-consciousness long ago, modern-day man can only describe and understand the concept of God according to their mental capabilities and inner limitations. How can the finite (human) understand the infinite (God)?

Every action is first manifested through a thought and one cannot experience their own Beingness without the act itself. Thought alone does not put one in a true state of Being. A thought only comes into Being by the act and the act becomes a reality only if there is at least one witness. This means that reality is only able to exist if there is an awareness or consciousness to perceive it.

A correctly built Pyramid with equilateral triangles on each external wall transmits necessary energy for the universe. The apex of the Pyramid signifies God, eternal power, and unity. Each vertex at the base of the Pyramid also signifies something specific. There are four vertices at the base of each Pyramid that represent the living (humans and animals), the plant life, the inanimate, and the spiritual, respectively. All four of the vertices are connected in a straight line to the apex of the Pyramid through the four sides of the Pyramid. Fatasol created the laser energy (EMLP) through the connection to the apex for the Divine connection according to their vision and understanding.

As mentioned before, the galactic communication with the eternal Light was continuous. I believe that even today there is a connection but perhaps using a different energetic connection without laser technology; perhaps through the bodies of the ancient Pharaohs who store the energy in their bodies up until today.

Spiritual laws and physical laws hold the foundations for building the Pyramids. Spirit is life and physical matter is its resistance. Spirit is radiation, and the physical matter is contrastive. Through the construction of the Pyramid, man is the link that connected the spirit world and the physical world. Without the resistance of the physical, creation as a whole would not be possible. The Pyramids, their secret tunnels, secret rooms, and the huge basements on which they sit were themselves the mother ships. Every pyramid can levitate by shrinking its base, flying to wherever it desires, and return back to its place as if nothing happened. This is material resistance. All of this is in the hands of the aliens (Fatasol) in whom lies the power of the mind, the power of thought, the secret of creation, and the complete understanding of the material world. Only with the proper combination and harmony between the laws of nature, such as the laws of physics and the laws of the spirit, is it possible to reach this level of power. The Hebrews were the builders of the Pyramids but the Pharaohs were the architects. Nothing was done out of force or by suffering. It was considered a privilege to the Hebrews to be part of this event in history. The Pyramid Code was not a secret at this point in time. As time passed, it turned to become a secret since the Pharaoh rulers abused the power given to them and were no longer to be trusted.

STRUCTURE OF THE PYRAMID

The pyramid consists of four equilateral triangular surfaces. Each triangle has three equal sides and three vertices. The inner surface within each of the triangles is known as the "Divine surface". God resides within each of the triangles (Divine surfaces) and is an integral part of the Pyramid. The four equilateral surfaces on the Pyramid allow us to understand that each Pyramid has four visible Divine surfaces projecting from the exterior of the Pyramid into the Universe, as well as four internal Divine surfaces radiating into the Pyramid. The base of the Pyramid is the basic Divine surface that consists of a square with four vertices. The square radiates its energy through its surface (both internal and external) as well as its four vertices to the apex at the top of the Pyramid. Each vertex at the base of the Pyramid faces a different direction; North, South, East, and West. Each wall (Divine surface) of the Pyramid also faces a different direction; North, South, East, and West. Each vertex at the base of the Pyramid provides energy for the living (human and animal), the plant life, the inanimate, and the spirit. All of these vertices, as one, radiate and absorb the Divine energy from the apex at the top of the Pyramid. The apex is always connected by laser or solar radiation to the original Divine energy (source). On all of the Divine surfaces and all of the vertices, energy radiates and absorbs the Divine energy simultaneously (the Pyramid both projects and receives energy). The Pyramid transmits through its Divine surfaces the Divine energy that radiates outward but also inward through its internal Divine surfaces. The Divine surface at the base of the pyramid radiates energy into the Pyramid upward to the apex (towards the spirit) and downward into the Earth (towards the physical).

When the Pyramid rises and flies as it did in the ancient days, one light could be seen coming out of the apex and four from the vertices on the base towards the North, South, East, and West. There were twelve lights at the bottom of the base Divine surface in the shape of a circle that could only be seen when flying. These lights symbolized the Zodiac. Additionally, there was one light in the middle of the circle that represented the Divine light. Even today, there are spaceships that exist in the shape of Pyramids exactly how I have described them here (spaceships exist in many shapes and styles such as pyramids, cylinders, saucers, flying triangles, and many other different shapes). There are mother-ships that look like massive industrialized cities that just hover in space waiting for incoming and outgoing flights. The size of each is unimaginable. Mother-ships usually hover in space without motion. They rarely move, hover and fly to different geographical locations.

Every Pyramid stores worldly power and Divine energy eternally due to the way the Pyramid was constructed by the Fatasol. Every Pyramid was built in different sizes but every wall is always at a 51-degree angle with a precise angle relative to the Sun. Each Pyramid is also connected to the twelve-star systems in our zodiac. As I said earlier, every Pyramid today is facing North towards the North star. The original Pyramids were built by Divine energetic powers, but have been preserved throughout the years by alien energy (Fatasol) through EMP and EMLP. The Pyramid personifies the reality of the Divine energy embodying itself in the material world. This Divine energy resides in every one of its creations as well as all the creations of other beings (aliens, Fatasol, or simply human beings). The four walls of the Pyramid personify, signify and symbolize the Divine revelation multiplied by four.

HEAVENLY WINDS & THE GARDEN OF EDEN

God radiates his influence in four different ways through four heavenly winds. The source of these energies (the four heavenly winds) comes from the Garden of Eden which is a paradise according to our understanding today. The Garden of Eden is located in Iraq, not far from Baghdad. It is a place that is exposed to the spirituality of the soul, however, it is hidden from the naked eye. The four characteristics of the flow of these winds (the heavenly winds) exist in everything that is created on Earth. Every wind has a feature as well as an influence. Western wind: brings rain, humidity, and warmth.

Eastern wind: brings coolness and refreshment.

Northern wind: brings cold and dryness.

Southern wind: brings the heat.

It's incredible that all four heavenly winds come from the same geographical location and the same energetic source, yet each wind holds within it a different characteristic. How could it be that warm air comes from the South and cold air comes from the North yet they are both coming from the same source, simultaneously? This is one of the secrets of creation!

HIDDEN MYSTICISM

Today, mysticism is hidden, but the day will come when the mysticism will be revealed and transparent. It will no longer be hidden. The Pyramid basically embodies everything that was, is, and will be. The Pyramid is the connection created by man between the physical and the spiritual. Other than the stone which is visible to the eye, a Pyramid is composed of the following base components:

18 laser lights symbolize life (which is represented by the number 18 in Hebrew) and Divine energy. (In Gematria, which is an alphanumeric code of assigning a numerical value to a word based on its letters, the word "Life", translated from Hebrew, is equal to the numerical value of 18).

10 internal and external surfaces symbolizing Divine physical and spiritual giving (the word "ten" in Hebrew means "to give" and also represents "wealth") between the creation and the Creator. (the numerical value of "10" always represents "1" which symbolizes **oneness**). **8** lines connecting the vertices through which energies flow infinitely between the base and the vertex (the number 8 symbolizes infinity).

5 vertices including the apex at the top of the Pyramid which represents the Divine (the numerical value of "5" represents the letter "Hay" in Hebrew which symbolizes the Divine God) connection that is connected to one's own Being.

4 vertices at the spiritual base (4 heavenly winds) that always point towards North, South, East and West.

The Zodiac is an integral part of the Earth and the Pyramids. Without the energetic radiance of the zodiac signs (constellations), the Earth and the Pyramids would never survive. The constellations of the Zodiac surround Earth and are fixed in space. The Zodiac constantly emits twelve different energies from its twelve different, fixed, constellations in the direction of Earth. Within the confines of each of the twelve constellations of the Zodiac exist twelve stars that are not visible to those who are not currently at the awareness of the upper levels of the 5th dimension or higher. The twelve stars within the confines of each constellation each spin on their own axis. Additionally, the twelve stars within the confines of each constellation all revolve around the centre of each constellation as a unit. This means that there are 144 stars within the confines of the constellations in the Zodiac that are not visible to the eye. These stars will only become visible to us when we reach the upper limits of the 5th dimension or higher. Earth's origin of creation is a direct result of the twelve different energies radiating from the twelve different constellations of the Zodiac in a circular (counter-clockwise) motion around the Earth. This resulted in the formation of the physical world. Earth grew into what we know it to be today via an intimate connection with the Sun and the solar energy emanating from the zodiac. This eventually turned Earth into a satellite of the Sun and today the Earth is an integral part of the Sun and the stars. The Earth is a physical creation that was created through the use of the energies of the stars (planets) and the Sun.

The zodiac is made up of 12 constellations. Each constellation is symbolized by an animal, inanimate object, or soul. Each of these symbolizes the spirit based on four fundamental points which are the four Divine areas of the heavens in a Divine being. These four fundamental points are:

1. Lion: symbolizing the Divine surface, Fire: The lion is a powerful symbol that is often used to represent the divine surface of fire. It is associated with strength, courage, and royalty, and is known to be a symbol of the sun and of divine power.

2. Eagle: (or scorpion according to today's astrologers) symbolizes the Divine surface, Wind: The eagle, or scorpion according to today's astrologers, is a symbol of the divine surface of wind. It is associated with freedom and soaring high above and is known to be a symbol of the sky and of the divine spirit

3. Bull: symbolizing the Divine surface, Earth: The bull is a symbol that is often linked to the divine surface of the earth. It is associated with strength, fertility, and determination, and is known to be a symbol of the land and of divine energy.

4. Aquarius: symbolizing the Divine surface, Water: Finally, Aquarius is a symbol of the divine surface of the water It is associated with creativity, intelligence, and innovation, and is known to be a symbol of the sea and of divine flow.

All four symbols are powerful representations of the divine, and each one brings its own unique message

As stated earlier, each Divine surface is a triangle with three vertices. Being that each Pyramid has four walls (Divine surfaces), when the number of vertices of each Divine surface (3) is multiplied by the number of walls on the Pyramid structure (4), we get the number 12. This represents the twelve different constellations within the Zodiac. Every constellation in the Zodiac has its own uniqueness:

Aries is often seen as a representation of libido, the force of the spring season, and the drive to act. Virgo, on the other hand, is seen as a representation of the mother of nature, a symbol of nurturing and caring for the world around us. There are many more examples of the symbolic roles of the zodiac signs. For instance, Gemini is associated with communication and interaction, Sagittarius with exploration, and Leo with leadership and courage. Cancer is considered a symbol of security and a protector of home and family, while Aquarius is associated with invention and creativity. Lastly, Scorpio is often seen as a representation of passion and intensity. Each of the zodiac signs serves as a reminder of the different forces that shape our lives and the world around us.

To sum up the essence of the Pyramid Code in a nutshell. Every Pyramid in the universe signifies Divine perfection, Divine spirituality, Divine physicality, and eternal Light. Every Pyramid moves behaves, transmits, and absorbs spiritual and physical energy through the use of basic principles at the source of the Pyramid *Being* (The Pyramid is a *Being*, as established). The physical Beingness of the Pyramid is the power of electricity.

The spiritual Beingness of the Pyramid is a powerful force that is derived from **the power of thought**. It is the source of great power and energy that transcends time and space. By tapping into this energy and directing it towards a particular purpose, we are able to manifest our desires in the physical realm. It is an energy that is greater than the sum of its parts and can be used to create a higher level of consciousness. When we use this energy in a positive way, it can help us to realize our dreams and bring us closer to our higher purpose. It is a universal force that we can all tap into and use to transform our lives.

The electricity that I am speaking of is not the same electricity that we know today. It is an electric force that exists in the hands of very few people. This force is not known to the scientists and ordinary people of today. Electricity has spiritual foundations but it is the material being of the Pyramid. Electricity is not seen by the naked eye and it has no taste, smell, or color. Electricity is not alive or inanimate, however, it can be measured by humans through certain devices that can determine its level of power. Electricity can kill or revive and build or destroy all at the will of the operator.

Electricity is the vital energy that is necessary for the survival of the Universe in all its frequencies and vibrations. Natural electricity, as opposed to artificial electricity (man-made), can provide us with infinite energy and comfort in the modern world that we live in. I am referring to universal free and natural electricity that does not pollute the Earth, the human body, or the soul. Modern-day artificial technology works at a frequency of **50HZ-60HZ** depending on the country in which the electricity is produced. The average Western country uses **400TWH** of electricity. There is a great deal of this artificial electricity that surrounds us at any given moment. This artificial poison is now essential for the survival of the population today. With such a poisonous creation, it is not surprising that the global frequency has gone astray, along with the frequency of the people living in it. Along with its advancement and comfort, it has also brought various physical and spiritual illnesses that significantly affect the power of thought and the soul. This has caused the modern man to go crazy. It has taken us out of consciousness.

Everything in the universe moves by electricity (energy) and electricity is an integral part of the entire universe. It is also essential to the various Beings who dwell in it and move within it through the use of vibration, frequency, and the power of thought. Electricity is part of our bodies. Every part of the body operates at different frequencies (such as the heart, kidney, lung, or brain). Although different parts of the body operate at different frequencies, the general frequency of the entire body as a whole is **7.83HZ.** It's interesting that the earth also works on a general frequency of **7.83HZ** which symbolizes life (**7+8+3=18** which symbolizes life in Hebrew through the connection of its letters in the Hebrew alphabet).

I highly doubt this to be a coincidence. Our bodies are electrical systems and our neural system acts as the wires that conduct electricity. This electricity vibrates throughout the body with the help of the water which is about 70% of the body.

It is important to note that the Earth is comprised of **70%** water, just like the human body. I cannot believe that this is mere chance.

The water vibrates at the frequency of **100THZ** which symbolizes the One **(1+0+0 = 1 which symbolizes Oneness)** that rules everything and anything. The Sun operates at a frequency of **5.9642GHZ.**

5+9+6+4+2 = 26

2+6 = 8

26 (which is the numerical value in Gematria for the word "Yehova", which means God in Hebrew) symbolizes the Divine power (God) which is infinite. 8 symbolizes infinity (just look at the symbol used for the number "8" itself. All of these numbers are according to the conversion from the Hebrew Alphabet (which was also used by the Pharaohs). I am compelled to believe that the conversion of all of these numbers is not a coincidence.

The entire universe and everything within the universe receive its life force and Beingness from natural electricity, which is incomprehensible to us. Scientists have yet to find the source that powers the heart, brain, Earth, or Sun which keeps us so vital. The fundamental

energy of naturally occurring electricity is the same fundamental energy that is intrinsic to thought, every living being, and the building and operation of the Pyramid. By becoming in tune with the constitutional energy behind naturally occurring electricity we can unlock the secrets behind creation and all that is sacred.

Thought precedes everything in the universe. Thought is an integral part of creation; the spiritual and the physical creation. Thought is the power that connects the entire universe including the connection between aliens, humans, animals, plants, Fatasol, and God himself. By the way, we humans are at the lowest level of consciousness before plants. Even animals have surpassed us. Humans today are at an extremely low level, far from the 5th dimension. Clean and pure thoughts bring us to eternal consciousness needed to activate not just the Pyramids, but the entire Universe. The Pyramid Code is part of the secret of the Universe; a secret that we will only reach with the right consciousness. Ever since the time of the Pharaohs, human beings were known as the people who contaminated the Fatasol race.

- Every Pyramid receives, provides, absorbs, transmits, and stores EMP and EMLP. Every Pyramid moves through the use of magnets in its base, the energy of the Sun, and the power of thought of its operators.
- Every Pyramid, regardless of its size or location, can fly to any distance regardless of space or time.
- Every Pyramid is built of stone (rock) that symbolizes the Divine surface, the Earth. Every Pyramid is built and set at a

specific angle (51 degrees) toward the zodiac, the Sun, and the North Star.

- Every Pyramid contains 18 laser lights that symbolize Divine energy and the Divine light with one always at the Apex and the rest at the base.
- Every Pyramid and its Divine surfaces are facing and are connected to the heavenly winds and their directions of North, South, East, and West.
- Every Pyramid is an independent spaceship and some have also served as motherships. Every Pyramid has a massive basement underneath it containing its tools, instruments, machines, and spaceships.
- Every Pyramid has hidden rooms and tunnels within it (especially underneath it). Every Pyramid contains its history and documentation (using the Hebrew alphabet) on its inner walls in the secret rooms that were engraved using laser technology. The engravings reveal the purpose of the Pyramids, the Pyramid Code, and the code that activates it.
- Every pyramid can also shrink by moving the stones and rocks at its base into the pyramid itself.
- Every Pyramid is independent without relying on one another; however, all are connected to the Eternal Light.
- Pyramids also exist as structures on other planets in the universe and they operate

with the same foundation as the ones on Earth, only with different levels of gravity which vary from planet to planet

- Pyramid can manipulate natural forces, such as gravity, in any way its operator desires.

THE PYRAMID STAR

Every star in the entire universe is a circle except for one star which is known as the Pyramid star. Like all other stars, it has been moving for eons in direct connection with the zodiac and its constellations, however, it is in the shape of a Pyramid. The Pyramid star contains life but not according to our limited understanding. Only worthy souls who meet the highest demands of the supreme power make it to the Pyramid Star. The Pyramid star and every Pyramid on Earth were made, created, and operated through the removal of time and space as well as combining the power of thought together with the physical technologies of EMP and EMLP.

THE POWER OF THOUGHT

The only thing in the entire universe that is faster than the speed of light and the speed of sound is thought. Aliens and human beings that operate spaceships (Pyramids) activate their crafts through thought combined with the energy of the body. For example, the operator of a spaceship uses his hands to protect his internal spiritual energy in order to propel a physical machine through the use of his thought. The main factor in the incomprehensible speed of spaceships today and in more ancient times is thought. It is important to note that Fatasol in ancient times thought on a much higher vibration and therefore and still are capable of performing physical acts that appear supernatural to us according to our limited understanding and awareness.

10
Chapter Ten

Sacred Secret:

"There is a treasure to be desired and oil in the dwelling of the wise, but a foolish man spendeth it up."-

The Greatest Human SECRET

In this final chapter, I will explore the Sacred Secret, unknown to many, that holds probably the most powerful knowledge ever known to humanity. This knowledge has been kept from humanity for thousands of years, and its importance is vital. It holds the power to unlock our greatest mental, emotional, and physical potential, and to help us achieve our highest goals.

This knowledge is not exclusive to any one culture or belief system. It transcends all boundaries, and its power is available to everyone. It is an expansive and holistic approach to life that can help us to become more conscious and self-aware. By connecting with this wisdom, we can access our own innate power and discover our true purpose in life.

Esoteric truth is an idea that has been discussed for centuries and is believed to be a hidden knowledge that comes from a higher power.

At the same time, a large amount of thinking has gone into the concept of sex without procreation. This is an idea that is relatively new but has been gaining traction in recent years. Sexual alchemy is a term that is often used to describe the process of sexual energy being used for transformative purposes. It is believed that this type of energy can be used to create powerful spiritual transformations.

Furthermore, there are 33 vertebrae in the human spine, and this number has been linked to the life of Jesus Christ. It is said that the 33 vertebrae represent the 33 years that Jesus lived on this earth. Additionally, the substance that comes from the medulla, which is the center of the brain, is said to look like the Ark of the Covenant. This symbolizes the connection between the physical and spiritual realms.

The story of Santa Claus is symbolic of the journey of our spiritual essence. The angel's wings signify the divine energy that surrounds us and the medulla is a representation of the divine spark that exists within us. This spark travels down our spine to our sacrum, where it is transformed into a physical form, becoming Christ. If we do not squander this essence, it ascends again, traveling back up to heaven. This is a metaphor for cultivating our spiritual essence and allowing it to ascend. This is why Santa Claus is said to come down the chimney - the chimney is a representation of the journey of the spiritual essence, and if we take care of it, it will ascend back to heaven.

The claustrum is often referred to as the 'gateway to consciousness', as it is believed to pass information between different areas of the brain. It is located between the insula and the temporal lobe, situated in the very center of the brain. Scientists have proposed that this is why the substance of Santa Claus is believed to pass through the chimney and back up, and why the claustrum is central to the brain. The claustrum is part of the cerebral cortex, and it has been found to be connected to many other areas of the brain. This includes the hippocampus, the amygdala, the basal ganglia, the thalamus, and the cerebellum. It is believed to be responsible for the integration of information from different parts of the brain, in order to form a cohesive whole. As such, the claustrum has been found to be important in the formation of higher cognitive functions, such as memory, learning, attention, and decision-making. This is why it is so important in the formation of consciousness, and why it is often referred to as the 'gateway to consciousness'.

The secretion of brain fluid, commonly referred to as "Christos" in ancient Greek, is a beautiful oil-like substance that originates from the cerebrum. It then passes down the spinal cord, eventually reaching the sacral plexus. This plexus is located right next to the sacrum - the five bottommost fused vertebrae at the end of the spinal column. It is believed that this fluid has healing properties, and has been used in traditional healing practices for centuries. Many believe that it can help to reduce inflammation, help to balance the body, and even aid in healing physical and emotional trauma. It is an important part of traditional healing practices and has become increasingly popular in recent years.

The Sacrum is composed of five fused bones and it is the bottommost part of the Spinal Cord. It is connected to the Sacral Plexus which is the source of the fluid that pours down the Spinal Cord from the Cerebrum. The Claustrum, otherwise known as the 'Holy Claustrum', produces and secretes a beautiful oil called the Christos. The word 'secret' is derived from this oil. This oil is believed to be a source of healing and spiritual power.

Our body has been designed in an amazing way, with the spinal cord acting as an extension of the brain. Not only does it help with movement, but it also does some thinking too. This is why the claustrum, otherwise known as the Santa Claus from the classic Christmas story, is considered sacred. This fluid that flows down to the plexus is a holy fluid, and it is from this story of Santa Claus bringing presents down the chimney that we get the metaphor. In essence, it is a way of telling the story of the power of the physiology of our bodies and how it enables us to do so much.

Every month, when the moon is in the sign where your son was when you were born, a germ or seed is planted in the solar plexus, which is just above the sacral plexus. This germ is the oil that Christ was born in Bethlehem. The solar plexus is otherwise known as Bethlehem and is where Christ was born. This oil needs to return each month as if it had come from Bethlehem. This fluid is a reminder of the grandeur of Christ's birth and the power of the moon's energy. The power of the fluid can help to bring peace, comfort, and harmony in your life.

The oil of Christ is said to have a powerful vibration that increases as it ascends the spinal cord. This oil is first differentiated in the pineal and pituitary glands, each of which holds an electric and magnetic charge, respectively. Once this process is complete, the oil is sent down the spinal cord and into the midbrain. Here, the oil is said to have a powerful effect on the body and mind, allowing for heightened spiritual awareness and spiritual growth. Thus, it is essential that the oil of Christ is able to make its way to the midbrain in order to reap the full benefits of its powerful vibration.

The magnetic portion of the oil is differentiated and brought down the spinal cord via the Pingala and the Eda nerves, which are also known as the Kundalini and the Kundabatha. It arrives at the sacral plexus, awaiting the germinating of the seed which happens once a month, 12 times a year. If we are able to transmute that seed and cause it to rise, as it rises in the spinal cord it reaches the medulla oblonga. This is an important process for cultivating spiritual energy and developing personal power.

The Tree of Life is an intricate web of nerves that starts at the spine and ascends through the medulla oblongata, pons, and midbrain, eventually reaching the vagus nerve also known as the pneumogastric nerve. This nerve descends from the brain, providing connections to the pineal and pituitary glands and also to the lungs and the stomach. By running through the body, this network of nerves helps to regulate the functions of the organs and systems and to maintain a healthy balance of the body's energy. It is through the Tree of Life that we can better understand the intricate connections of our body and how it works to keep us alive.

The Ancients had a deep understanding of the power of the Christ seed, born in Bethlehem every month. They believed that abstaining from sexual activity during this period would conserve the oil and Seed, allowing it to ascend to a higher vibration. This vibration would travel from the heart chakra to the throat chakra, bursting through and allowing the oil to reach its highest potential. This ancient wisdom has been passed down through the generations, and can still be practiced today.

The power of human behavior is undeniable in our ability to alter the vibratory rate of our own life force. By engaging in practices like meditation, mindful breathing, and eating healthy, we can raise our vibrations to higher frequencies. This is powerful because, as we raise our vibrations, we are able to cross the vagus nerve, located at the top of the spinal column. This is particularly special because the 33 vertebrae of the spinal column represent the age at which Jesus was crucified. When the oil, or life force, reaches the very top, we become fully connected to the source energy and reach a higher level of consciousness. The potential of such practices is immense and should not be ignored.

Because of the crucifixion of Christ at 33 years of age, when the oil arrives at the very top, it waits to reach the optic thalamus, which is an egg-shaped organ located in the middle of the head. When it crosses the pneumogastric nerve, this is known as the crucifixion. The oil is not killed or destroyed, however, it is magnified 1,000 times and touches the optic thalamus. This magnified oil then continues to pass through the nervous system, activating the body's energy centers, and it begins to dissolve all negative energy and feelings. This allows the individual to experience a heightened spiritual consciousness, leading to a more meaningful and fulfilling life.

The oil then touches the optic thalamus and for two and a half days remains in a condition that is called Dead. This state is considered to be a form of death, after which it reaches the pineal gland. The Egyptians and the Greeks referred to the optic thalamus as the light of the world because they understood its role in the body. They were aware that the oil, after touching the thalamus, would move to the pineal gland and illuminate it. This illumination is what gives the body the ability to experience spiritual awakening and enlightenment. Thus, the Egyptians and the Greeks were able to use the optic thalamus and the pineal gland to achieve a spiritual connection with the divine.

This precious oil descended from the claustrum of the cerebrum, was differentiated in the pineal and pituitary glands, and descended the spinal cord. It was known that, eventually, this oil would ascend. The enlightened portion of mankind had the ability to cause the oil to ascend to the optic thalamus, which in turn caused a million brain cells to be lightened. This precious oil was a symbol of hope to many and its ascension was celebrated by all. The knowledge of this oil will continue to be passed down from generation to generation, reminding us that we too can ascend to a higher level.

The Ancients understood the importance of preserving the life-giving oil within each one of us and warned of the dangers of depleting it. When we overexert ourselves with activities such as overeating, drinking alcohol, or engaging in sexual activities at the wrong time, it has a detrimental effect on the seed of life within us. This is often referred to as "eating from the Tree of Life" because when the oil is depleted, the physical body begins to die. In essence, our actions can have a direct impact on our health and longevity. That is why it is so important to take care of ourselves and practice moderation in all that we do.

The oil that descends from the cerebrum is known otherwise as the manna from Heaven, as heaven means to be heaved up and the cranium, or the dome, sits atop the torso which was referred to as the heavens. The heart area and heart chakra was known as the Midgard or the Middle Garden, and the generative area was known as Sodom and Gomorrah, the area of Desire, both animal and other. This oil is believed to be a miraculous blessing from Heaven, as it is believed to be the source of a person's power, creativity, and intuition.

Whereas, the Garden of Eden is a symbol of abundance, and the 'land flowing with milk and honey' is often thought to refer to the bounty of the physical world. In fact, the reference may be to the pineal gland, which produces a secretion known as honey that contains dimethyltryptamine (DMT). Similarly, the pituitary gland produces a secretion known as milk. It is believed that this secret knowledge of the pituitary and pineal glands is what is referred to in the land flowing with milk and honey in the Bible. This is a sacred secret because the secretion that comes from the Sacral plexus is one of the most important aspects of the human body. Together, the pituitary and pineal glands form the basis of the spiritual and physical connection between the mind and body that is essential for overall well-being.

The Ancients believed strongly in the power of the seed, and its ability to extend life. They kept the secrets of the seed closely guarded and passed it down through generations. To ensure that the seed was kept safe, the Egyptians built Ascension Chambers and pyramids and taught the science of respecting and protecting the seed. The Gospels also contain many references to the seed and its importance, and give detailed instructions on how to look after and guard it. Through this guarded and respected seed, they believed that it was possible to extend life and achieve immortality.

I, the Light of the World, proclaim that those who follow me shall not walk in darkness. The optic Thalamus is the Light of the World, so keep your eyes simple and open. For if your eye is dark, your whole body will be dark. This eye has been known throughout time as the Third Eye and is in fact a spiritual eye.

For those who deny this, it is likely due to their religious beliefs. Most churchgoers will deny this because they view Jesus Christ as a historical person only. However, the truth is that the Light of the World is within each and every one of us, and that is something that should be embraced by all.

Jesus spoke of the sacred mystery of the Christ who dwells within us, for the Kingdom of God is not something that can be seen and touched, but something that exists within us. He tells us not to look for it externally, for there will be those who will try to deceive us and lead us astray, saying "Look, here he is, or there." Jesus was very clear in his words that the Kingdom of God is something that exists within us, and can only be found within.

If one is to elevate their energy and get out of the lower chakras, it is essential to understand the implications of the lower chakras. The lower chakras are associated with sexuality, strife, envy, power, greed, wealth, and all the materialistic desires of life. By constantly indulging in these desires and feeding off the fruit of the tree of life, one is neglecting the pneumogastric nerve system. This nerve system is responsible for carrying the oil back to the higher chakras, which can help one elevate their energy and achieve spiritual and emotional growth. Therefore, if one is to raise their energy and get out of the bottom chakras, it is important to understand the implications of the lower chakras and to consciously abstain from feeding off the fruit of the tree of life.

The cerebrum is the largest and uppermost part of the brain and is hollowed out. The midbrain and the limbic system, situated at the top of the spinal cord, are considered to be the “holy of holies” within the brain. The cerebellum, located at the back of the brain, is often referred to as the “small brain”. The cerebrum is associated with the sign of Aries, while the cerebellum is associated with Taurus. The left brain is considered to be the masculine side, while the right brain is considered to be the feminine. These two hemispheres of the brain are connected by the corpus callosum.

The idea of the God-Man being the cerebrum and the Adam Man being the cerebellum has been around for thousands of years. This oil, which has been preserved and conserved, is essential in order for it to reach the optic thalamus. When the oil does reach the optic thalamus, it generates new blood in the body, preventing it from becoming old and toxic. This process must occur in order for us to maintain our health and vitality.

Raising the oil to the optic Thalamus can be a way to promote healing by reactivating millions of dormant brain cells that are present in everyone's brain. This is why when you go to the shopping mall, you might notice people who appear to be zombies, or zombified, as they have not received the oil. This oil is necessary for brain stimulation and thus people with a lack of it will often display zombie-like behavior. By raising the oil to the optic Thalamus, more people can experience the healing effects of this oil and become aware of their surroundings once again.

In the Bible, this is known as tithing: returning one-tenth to the Lord. It is a reminder of the importance of the Lord and of the power of gold. It symbolizes how we can turn lead into gold, just as we can turn ignorance into enlightenment and consciousness. This is why we are able to raise the condition of our oil, as it climbs the spine and ascends. Just as a thermometer rises with warmth, so too does our knowledge rise, leading us to a higher level of understanding. This is why the Bible instructs us to return one tenth to the Lord, as a reminder of this journey of transformation.

When the vibration of the body is raised at the top of the spine where the pneumogastric nerve is crossed, it does not mean death, but rather multiplication. Physical regeneration is a result of this, but spiritual regeneration is also possible. By raising the vibration in this way, one can experience the power of the higher mind and clairvoyance. Mediumship also occurs in the solar plexus when the vibration is raised in this manner. With this process, one can tap into a higher power and a greater potential for spiritual growth.

The human body contains four distinct brains: the cerebrum, otherwise known as the 'God Brain', the cerebellum, known as the 'Man Brain', the medulla oblongata, responsible for involuntary actions such as breathing and blood circulation, and the fourth brain, the solar plexus. This fourth brain is more closely related to the instinctive animal brain, and it is capable of receiving images from the ether, from the air, in a similar way to animals.

Raising the oil is of utmost importance in order to escape the lower mind which is the solar plexus. This is a secret known to the elites, and they have ruthlessly persecuted those who teach the truth of the Ascension process and the Christ within. They have labelled these individuals as Heretics, renegades, and unbelievers in an attempt to keep the truth from being revealed. But in spite of their efforts, the truth of the Ascension process and the Christ within is still alive and can be accessed by those who are willing to raise the oil and learn the truth. It is this truth that will ultimately enable one to ascend to a higher level of consciousness.

The story of Christ and the Ascension process is a story of profound significance. It is a story of rising up to a higher place, a place of spiritual transformation and growth. This process is often referred to as the 'heavenly ascent'. In the Bible, God instructs Moses to build the Ark of the Covenant with two cherubim above it, covering it over. The two cherubim that are mentioned in the Bible are said to represent the two flaps of the cerebrum, otherwise known as the Caribbean. This is why the cerebrum is often referred to as the Dome of Heaven. This is symbolic of the Ascension process, which is the journey of rising up to a higher place, a place that is closer to the divine. Through this process, one ascends to the heavenly realm, a place of peace and enlightenment. This is the power of the Ascension process and the true story of the Christ within.

The Law of God is written on the two tablets, and they contain the basic principles and tenets of our faith. But there is something even greater that is hidden within the depths of our being, and that is the Optic Thalamus, which is the Ark of the Covenant. Within this sacred chamber lies the Limbic System and the Midbrain, the Pons, the Medulla Oblongata, and the Pineal Gland. These are the Holy of Holies, and it is here that we must return the good oil in the middle of our heads. This is known as the Hippocampus, and it represents the White Horse that Jesus rides. By connecting to this divine energy, we can access the highest levels of truth and knowledge, and live our lives in accordance with the Law of God.

Amon's Horn is an anatomical feature located in the middle of the head. It is believed to be named after the Egyptian god Amon, and it is composed of the claustrum, cerebrum, cerebellum, midbrain, optic thalamus, and pineal gland. These structures are said to be covered by the Cherubim, the Angels of God. It is believed that when we invoke the name of Jesus, our prayers are said to be heard through these structures. This is why Amon's Horn is such an important anatomical feature in the human body.

The midbrain and the optic Thalamus, as well as the pineal gland and the pituitary gland, otherwise known as Joseph and Mary, are responsible for sending oil down the spinal cord. These two await the return of their son, who is born in Bethlehem. The solar plexus is activated once a month, and if it is over-stimulated by living in excess or consuming too much alcohol, it can result in riotous behavior.

The cerebrum is the source of the oil that is essential for life. It is a beautiful, crystalline dew that descends from the heavens and is secreted in the holy land. This oil is the secret of Christ, and without it, the human organism will die. It is a sacred fluid that nourishes and sustains us, and without it, life as we know it would not be possible. It is vital that we protect this precious oil, for it is our lifeblood. We must be mindful of the poisons that can dry it up, for without it, life will cease to exist.

The Holy Land is the body and the Jordan River is its spinal cord. These two are intrinsically connected, much like Jesus, who was baptized at the age of 30 and crucified at the age of 33. This connection is further emphasized by the degrees of the spinal cord, which correspond to the bones of the vertebrae. As we progress through life, we get our degrees and graduate with high honors. This is why the Jordan River is so important to us - it symbolizes the journey we all take to reach our ultimate goals in life.

If we stay in the sacrum, the sacred place that Jacob called the pineal, then we can understand the importance of Jacob's Ladder. Jacob laid his head upon a stone, which was actually the five fused bones of the sacrum, the place where the seed is born. If we can wrestle with the angel, as Jacob did, and receive a name change, like Jacob who became Israel, then we can come closer to God and see His face-to-face. That is the power of Jacob's Ladder, and it is through this power that we can better understand the divine.

The Christ within is the embodiment of the divine within each of us. It is the power of the soul transcending the physical body to connect with the spiritual universe. The body is the temple in which Christ resides and is composed of a myriad of complex systems and structures. The brain is the most powerful organ in the body, controlling our thoughts and emotions. The heart acts as a pump for the circulatory system, delivering vital nutrients to the body's cells. The generative system produces hormones and other compounds that help regulate bodily functions. The limbic system is responsible for our moods and behaviors. The nervous system helps us respond to the environment, sending signals to the brain and other parts of the body. The musculoskeletal system provides structure and movement. The lymphatic system helps to remove toxins from the body. All of these components work together to create the miraculous being that is the human body, and the embodiment of the divine within us.

The Sacred Secret is a powerful tool for transformation, and its impact is undeniable. It can help us to live more meaningful lives, and to create positive and lasting change in the world. By unlocking this ancient knowledge, we can unleash the power of the human spirit and gain access to the true potential of our souls.

CONCLUSION

Accessing the portal of higher energy

Man is the only creature on Earth who takes life too seriously. We get stuck in our own judgments and the judgments of others. We don't even realize the more things we judge, the more we attract. We attract everything we judge until we no longer judge what we have attracted. It's a cycle that we get stuck in, but it's all just a game that the gods created for fun. It's time to take a step back and realize that we can free ourselves from this cycle and enjoy life for what it is.

What we are experiencing in this world is stranger than any fiction story that we can ever imagine. It is a reminder of our Divinity - one that is so much broader and infinitely more significant than we can comprehend. We have willingly come here to this place to experience all of these things, and it is through the intensity of the feelings that we have, the emotions, and the senses that we are able to truly appreciate the beauty and magnificence of our world. We are here to learn and grow, to connect with others, and to discover the deeper truths of life. In recognizing this, we can better understand our place in the Universe and the power of our collective consciousness. We can come to accept the past and create a brighter future, one that is filled with love, joy, and peace.

We can live and experience what other people feel and thus, understand who we are and why we do the things we do. This repetition can be found in cycles that we often find ourselves in and it can be difficult to recognize and break out of these cycles. However, when we realize that we are in a cycle and start doing things differently, we can open ourselves up to new possibilities and opportunities. This can be seen in the way we play games or take on new challenges. By living differently and trying something new, we can find ourselves in a new world of adventure and exploration.

Leela, as it's referred to by Buddhists, is an experience of being able to play in the illusion of this world, to realize that you've been dreaming, and to live out the aspects of your hero's journey associated with that new level of dimensional perception. It's like lucid dreaming, but instead of just being aware that you're in a dream, you can actively participate in it. With Leela, you can explore the depths of your own subconscious, discover new potentials and capabilities, and ultimately become the best version of yourself. It's an incredibly powerful tool for personal growth and transformation. With Leela, you can make your own reality, and be the hero of your own story.

Realizing that we are the Creators of our own destiny is indeed a big shift. It leads us to understand why people make the choices they do;

what may be someone's trash can be someone else's treasure. But if we are playing a game, what is the point of having an epic death if we know that death is not real? Would we still choose to do the same things that we do in this life, or would we alter our course? It's a thought-provoking concept and one that is worth exploring.

Leela is an interesting concept, one that suggests that if we are constantly looking to help people who are constantly victimized, we may end up becoming victims ourselves. This is a difficult realization to come to and can turn our worldview upside down. We may then start to question many of the judgements we have made in the past and think about how we can use our actions to make a difference and not be complicit in further victimization. It's an important concept to consider, and one that could have a major impact on how we view and interact with the world.

It's easy to get stuck in the same cycles of Samsara, but it's possible to break free. We can learn to love and accept our destiny and path and realize that everything is connected. Every person we meet and every experience we have is a divine gift. Instead of asking "Why did the universe do this to me?" we can ask ourselves "What did this experience teach me?" This can shift our thinking and our perspective, allowing us to be open to the gifts the universe has to offer us. When we can see the divine in every experience, we can start to fall in love with our destiny.

We have chosen Amor Fati, the love of Destiny, as our principle, hoping to learn and fall in love with it. We believe in coincidences and might make right, and that willpower can create whatever it is we want. We also tend to think there is a juxtaposition between willpower and Destiny, though what we call Destiny is free power. This principle helps us to understand that our actions are important, but so is the greater force of the universe. We do not have full control over our lives and our destinies, but we can choose our attitudes, intentions, and actions, and that is what matters in the end.

This quote from an unknown origin speaks to the power of both the heart and the mind to find our true destiny. When we use both of these qualities together, the river of wisdom can carry us to the place we are meant to be. Our heart is our anchor, the source of our intuition, and the mind is our navigator, helping us to make sense of the world around us. When we combine these two forces, we can use the river of wisdom to take us to our destiny.

Our heart and mind are two forces that can come together to create something beautiful and powerful. When we take the time to listen to our hearts and use our minds to make sense of the world, the river of wisdom can be a powerful tool to help us get to where we are meant to go. Our destiny is within reach when we use both the heart and the mind together.

Learning to surrender to our destiny can be a difficult thing to accept, but it is often the wisest course of action. Our hearts contain a type of brain tissue, known as the sinoatrial node, which serves as the gateway to understanding unconditional love. While this love is often the most rewarding, it is also the most difficult to achieve. In order to learn how to accept and give unconditional love, we must also be willing to accept betrayal and judge those who do not fulfil our expectations. By learning to surrender to our destiny we can find the unconditional love we seek, and the places we were always meant to go.

We often forget that we are all connected by an unconditional love that transcends our physical boundaries. We are all connected by a force that is much deeper than our thoughts or our physical bodies. This force is our higher selves or subconscious sides, which are always trying to communicate with us. It is up to us to remove the veil that separates us from this higher self or subconscious side. This veil is self-imposed, and it can be difficult to recognize and breakthrough. However, when we make the effort to break through this veil, we can gain a greater understanding of our true selves and the unconditional love that binds us all.

Walter Russell said it best: Genius is self-bestowed and mediocrity is self-inflicted. By making judgments about ourselves, we open up the possibility to expand our perception and experience our inner genius or limit ourselves by making it separate from us. This is only embodied through the heart, brain, and consciousness. It is through our own self-reflection that we are able to make these judgments and have the potential to open our minds to something greater. We have the power to choose our own destiny and decide whether to embrace our inner genius or confine it. It is a choice that each of us faces, and it can make all the difference.

Accessing higher wisdom is a journey that transcends the polarity of the world. By expanding our perception and rising above the mundane, we open ourselves to greater knowledge. When we reach this level of understanding, we gain wisdom that can be used to navigate our lives and make better decisions. This wisdom is a portal to a higher level of understanding, clarity, and peace. By cultivating this knowledge and continuing to seek greater understanding, we can discover a life of joy and abundance.

The role of the sinoatrial node is one that is often overlooked, yet it is actually one of the last parts of the brain to develop. Many may not realize that the heart actually has its own 'brain', allowing us to think with our hearts rather than just our heads. The 'Heart Brain' allows us to access the heart aspect, which is located at the top of our hearts. We are able to use this to think beyond the logical and rational and to access more of our inner selves. This can be incredibly powerful, allowing us to make decisions not only based on our rational minds but also from our hearts.

The corpus callosum is an important part of our anatomy, as it is the connective tissue that separates the left and right brains. It is believed to be the bridge between the two hemispheres, allowing for communication between them. By tapping into this bridge, we can access a higher level of awareness and creativity. Really tapping into this bridge requires us to be deeply in tune with our emotions, going beyond the physical realm and into the spiritual. This connection can be felt by focusing on the area of the brain just above the brow which is often referred to as the third eye. This connection allows us to reach a state of heightened consciousness and open ourselves to new ideas and possibilities. It is said to be as if there is a specific geometry for this type of connection, allowing for a greater understanding of the world. With practice, we can use this connection to gain insight and clarity from within, bringing us closer to our true selves.

Surrendering to the Universe's divine plan and wisdom is a powerful way to tap into our true potential. When we are connected to the Universe rather than separate from it, we can finally move away from fighting against it. This is because we come to realize that the Universe is not happening to us, it is happening for us. When we accept this fact, we open ourselves up to the endless possibilities and potential that the Universe holds for us. We begin to understand that the Universe is our greatest ally and that it is working in our favor.

This understanding brings a sense of peace, as we are no longer fighting against the Universe, but rather, working with it. By surrendering to the Universe and its plan and wisdom, we open ourselves up to a world of abundance and serenity.

If you want to see the Joy; Be the Joy
If you want to see the Love; Be the Love

END

Ingram Content Group UK Ltd.
Milton Keynes UK
UKHW021813240723
425688UK00016B/91

9 781916 696433